simply
chocolate

simply chocolate

100 no fuss recipes for everyday cooking

First published in 2011

LOVE FOOD is an imprint of Parragon Books Ltd

Parragon
Chartist House
15-17 Trim Street
Bath BA1 1HA, UK

www.parragon.com

ISBN: 978-1-4454-5409-2

Printed in China

Introduction by Linda Doeser
New recipes and cover food styling by Teresa Goldfinch
Cover photography by Clive Streeter
Additional photography by Mike Cooper
Additional food styling by Lincoln Jefferson

This book uses imperial, metric, and US cup measurements. Follow the same units of measurement throughout; do not mix imperial and metric. All spoon measurements are level: teaspoons are assumed to be 5 ml, and tablespoons are assumed to be 15 ml. Unless otherwise stated, milk is assumed to be whole, eggs are large, individual vegetables, such as potatoes, are medium, and pepper is freshly ground black pepper.

The times given are an approximate guide only. Preparation times differ according to the techniques used by different people and the cooking times may also vary from those given as a result of the type of oven used. Optional ingredients, variations, or serving suggestions have not been included in the calculations.

Recipes using raw or very lightly cooked eggs should be avoided by infants, the elderly, pregnant women, convalescents, and anyone with a chronic condition. Pregnant and breast-feeding women are advised to avoid eating peanuts and peanut products. People with nut allergies should be aware that some of the prepared ingredients used in the recipes in this book may contain nuts. Always check the package before use.

Contents

Introduction

If you ask any gathering of people to list their 10 favorite cakes, cookies, desserts, and sweet treats, you can be sure that almost everyone will include at least one chocolate confection. It won't always be the same thing and, undoubtedly, there will be a few lists where chocolate features in all 10 choices, but there is no question of its popularity with adults and children alike. It's not simply the rich taste of chocolate that makes it so well loved. It also combines superbly with a lot of other ingredients that complement or contrast—sweet-sour dark cherries, tangy citrus, aromatic mint, spicy ginger, mellow rum, and refreshing coffee, for example—to create an abundance of tremendously indulgent recipes.

As a flavoring on its own or combined with other ingredients, chocolate is wonderfully versatile. It is equally delicious in luscious hot desserts and melt-in-your-mouth chilled ones and makes fabulous ice cream. It's great in quick and easy-to-make muffins, brownies, cookies, and cupcakes, while chocolate layer cakes and cheesecakes are always extra special. It's the perfect choice for sweetmeats and petits fours and, of course, makes marvelous shakes and warming chocolate drinks.

Chocolate comes from the cocoa bean, which grows on a tropical tree of the genus *Theobroma,* meaning "food of the gods." Its production is a lengthy and complicated process resulting in a variety of grades and types of chocolate. Bittersweet chocolate and semisweet chocolate have the strongest flavor and are less sweet than milk chocolate, which contains more sugar and also dry milk solids and milk fats. Strictly speaking, white chocolate isn't chocolate at all, because it's made from sweetened cocoa butter but no other elements of the cocoa bean, and it is technically known as white confectionery coating. All are used in cooking.

Unsweetened cocoa is also a common ingredient, especially in light yellow cakes, because it still has the lovely chocolate flavor but contains a lot less fat. It is also sometimes used in addition to chocolate to intensify the flavor.

Chocolate chips, which may be made from any type of chocolate, contain less cocoa butter than bars and so keep their shape during baking. They are, therefore, particularly well suited to cookies, although they feature in other recipes too. They are available in a variety of sizes but ½ inch/1 cm diameter may be the most useful.

Top Tips for Success

- It is always worth paying the extra cost for good-quality chocolate. Look for at least 70 percent cocoa in bittersweet chocolate and 50 percent in semisweet and milk chocolate. Similarly, more expensive, good-quality unsweetened cocoa has a more intense flavor than cheaper brands.
- Always store chocolate in its foil wrapping in a cool, dry place, ideally at 59–63°F/15–17°C. Keep it away from strong-smelling foods because it easily absorbs aromas.
- Do not store chocolate in the refrigerator unless absolutely necessary because it may acquire a harmless white bloom from absorbing moisture. It can also become oily when removed from the refrigerator if the kitchen is hot.
- Never melt chocolate over direct heat unless it is mixed with other ingredients, such as milk or cream. In that case, stir the mixture frequently until the chocolate has melted, then remove immediately from the heat.
- To melt chocolate, break it into pieces and put them into a heatproof bowl. Set the bowl over a saucepan of barely simmering water, but do not let the bottom of the bowl touch the surface of the water. Stir occasionally but be gentle to avoid splashing water into the bowl, which makes the chocolate granular. Remove from the heat as soon as the chocolate has melted. Do not cover the bowl or condensation will form.
- To melt chocolate in the microwave, break it into pieces and put them into a microwave-safe bowl. Heat on full power for 30 seconds, then stir to check whether the chocolate has melted—it will retain its shape so you can't tell by just looking. Continue to heat in bursts of 30 seconds until almost all the chocolate has melted, then remove from the microwave. The residual heat will melt the remainder. Melt white chocolate on medium power.
- Unsweetened cocoa has no added sugar so it is bitter tasting, while drinking chocolate mixes consist of about 75 percent sugar and are not suitable for baking.
- When using melted chocolate to decorate cookies or cakes, handle it as little as possible to avoid leaving unsightly fingerprints.
- Always sift unsweetened cocoa when adding it to mixtures to aerate it and remove any lumps. Recipes will often suggest sifting flour, unsweetened cocoa, and any leavening agents together to mix them.

1

Gorgeous Cakes & Cookies

double chocolate frosted cake

SERVES 10

1 cup butter, softened, plus extra for greasing

generous 1 cup superfine sugar

4 eggs, beaten

1½ cups self-rising flour

½ cup unsweetened cocoa

a little milk (optional)

filling

generous 1 cup heavy cream

8 oz/225 g white chocolate, broken into pieces

frosting

12 oz/350 g semisweet chocolate, broken into pieces

½ cup butter

scant ½ cup heavy cream

to decorate

4 oz/115 g semisweet chocolate curls

2 tsp confectioners' sugar and unsweetened cocoa, mixed

1 To make the filling, put the cream in a saucepan and heat to almost boiling. Put the white chocolate in a food processor and chop. With the motor running, pour the hot cream through the feed tube and process for 10–15 seconds, until smooth. Transfer to a bowl and let cool, then cover with plastic wrap and chill in the refrigerator for 2 hours, or until firm. Beat until just starting to hold soft peaks.

2 Preheat the oven to 350°F/180°C. Grease and line the bottom of an 8-inch/20-cm round deep cake pan with parchment paper. Put the butter and sugar in a bowl and beat until light and fluffy. Gradually beat in the eggs. Sift the flour and cocoa into a bowl, then fold into the mixture, adding milk, if necessary, to make a dropping consistency.

3 Spoon the batter into the prepared pan and bake in the preheated oven for 45–50 minutes, until a toothpick inserted into the center comes out clean. Let stand in the pan for 5 minutes, then transfer to a wire rack to cool completely.

4 To make the frosting, put the semisweet chocolate in a heatproof bowl set over a saucepan of gently simmering water until melted. Stir in the butter and cream. Let cool, stirring occasionally until the mixture is a thick spreading consistency. Slice the cake horizontally into 3 layers. Sandwich the layers together with the white chocolate filling. Cover the top and sides of the cake with the frosting and arrange the chocolate curls over the top. Sift the mixed confectioners' sugar and cocoa over the cake.

chocolate orange bundt cake

SERVES 8–10

2 small oranges

3 oz/85 g semisweet chocolate

1⅔ cups self-rising flour

1½ tsp baking powder

¾ cup butter, softened, plus extra for greasing

scant 1 cup superfine sugar

3 eggs, beaten

topping

1½ cups confectioners' sugar

2 tbsp orange juice

2 oz/55 g semisweet chocolate, broken into pieces

1 Preheat the oven to 325°F/160°C. Grease a 3¾-cup fluted Bundt pan or plain tube pan.

2 Grate the rind from one of the oranges and set aside. Pare the rind from the other orange and set aside. Cut the skin and pith from the oranges, then cut them into segments by cutting down between the membranes with a sharp knife. Chop the segments into small pieces, reserving as much juice as possible. Grate the chocolate coarsely onto a plate.

3 Sift the flour and baking powder into a bowl. Add the butter, superfine sugar, eggs, grated orange rind, and any reserved juice from the oranges. Beat until the batter is smooth. Fold in the chopped oranges and grated chocolate. Spoon the batter into the prepared pan and bake in the preheated oven for 40 minutes, or until well risen and golden brown. Let cool in the pan for 5 minutes, then turn out onto a wire rack to cool completely.

4 To make the topping, sift the confectioners' sugar into a bowl and stir in enough orange juice to make a coating consistency. Using a spoon, drizzle the icing over the cake. Put the chocolate in a heatproof bowl set over a saucepan of gently simmering water until melted. Drizzle the melted chocolate over the cake. Cut the reserved pared orange rind into thin strips and scatter over the cake. Let set before serving.

chocolate banana cake

SERVES 10–12

1 tsp sunflower oil, for oiling

2 ripe bananas (about 1½ cups when peeled and sliced)

2 tbsp lemon juice

¾ cup butter or margarine, softened

¾ cup light brown sugar

2 eggs, beaten

1½ cups self-rising flour

½ cup chopped pecans, plus extra pecan halves to decorate

2 oz/55 g semisweet chocolate, broken into pieces

2¾ oz/75 g white chocolate, broken into pieces

1 Preheat the oven to 350°F/180°C. Lightly oil and line the bottom of a 9 x 5 x 3-inch/23 x 13 x 8-cm loaf pan with parchment paper.

2 Cut the bananas into pieces, add the lemon juice, and mash to form a puree. Set aside.

3 Cream the butter with the sugar until light and fluffy, then gradually beat in the eggs, adding a little flour after each addition. When both eggs have been added, stir in the mashed bananas and then the remaining flour. Add the chopped pecans. Melt the semisweet chocolate in a heatproof bowl set over a saucepan of gently simmering water. Stir until smooth, then stir lightly into the cake batter.

4 Spoon the cake batter into the prepared pan and bake in the preheated oven for 45–55 minutes, or until a toothpick inserted into the center comes out clean. Remove from the oven and let cool slightly in the pan before turning out onto a wire rack to cool completely.

5 Melt the white chocolate in a heatproof bowl set over a saucepan of gently simmering water. Stir until smooth, then drizzle over the cooled cake. Arrange the pecan halves on top and let the chocolate set before serving.

white chocolate coffee gâteau

SERVES 8–10

3 tbsp unsalted butter, plus extra for greasing

3 oz/85 g white chocolate

⅔ cup superfine sugar

4 extra-large eggs, beaten

2 tbsp very strong black coffee

1 tsp vanilla extract

generous 1 cup all-purpose flour

frosting

6 oz/175 g white chocolate

6 tbsp unsalted butter

generous ½ cup sour cream

generous 1 cup confectioners' sugar, sifted

1 tbsp coffee liqueur or very strong black coffee

1 Preheat the oven to 350°F/180°C. Grease 2 x 8-inch/20-cm layer cake pans and line the bottoms with parchment paper. Place the butter and chocolate in a bowl set over a saucepan of hot water over low heat until just melted. Stir to mix lightly, then remove from the heat. Place the superfine sugar, eggs, coffee, and vanilla extract in a large bowl set over a saucepan of hot water and beat hard with an electric mixer until the mixture is pale and thick enough to leave a trail when the beaters are lifted.

2 Remove from the heat, sift in the flour, and fold in lightly and evenly. Quickly fold in the butter-and-chocolate mixture, then divide the batter between the prepared pans. Bake in the preheated oven for 25–30 minutes, until risen, golden brown, and springy to the touch. Let cool in the pans for 2 minutes, then turn out onto a wire rack.

3 For the frosting, place the chocolate and butter in a bowl set over a saucepan of hot water and heat gently until melted. Remove from the heat, stir in the sour cream, then add the confectioners' sugar and coffee liqueur and mix. Chill the frosting until thick and glossy. Use one-third of the frosting to sandwich the cakes together, then spread the rest over the top and sides.

Step 1

Step 2

Step 3

black forest gâteau

SERVES 8

2 lb/900 g fresh cherries, pitted and halved, plus whole fresh cherries, to decorate

1¼ cups superfine sugar

scant ½ cup cherry brandy

¾ cup all-purpose flour

5 tbsp unsweetened cocoa

½ tsp baking powder

4 eggs

3 tbsp unsalted butter, melted, plus extra for greasing

4 cups heavy cream

grated semisweet chocolate

1 Preheat the oven to 350°F/180°C. Grease and line a 9-inch/23-cm round springform cake pan with parchment paper.

2 Place the halved cherries in a saucepan, add 3 tablespoons of the sugar and the cherry brandy, and bring to a simmer over medium heat. Simmer for 5 minutes. Drain, reserving the syrup.

3 In a large bowl, sift together the flour, cocoa, and baking powder. Place the eggs in a heatproof bowl and beat in ¾ cup of the remaining sugar. Place the bowl over a saucepan of simmering water and beat for 6 minutes, or until thickened. Remove from the heat, then gradually fold in the flour mixture and melted butter.

4 Spoon into the prepared cake pan and bake in the preheated oven for 40 minutes. Remove from the oven and let cool in the pan.

5 Turn out the cake and cut in half horizontally. Mix the cream and the remaining sugar together and whip lightly until soft peaks form. Spread the reserved syrup over the cut sides of the cake, then top with half the whipped cream. Arrange the cherry mixture over the bottom half of the cake, then place the other half on top. Cover the top of the cake with the remaining whipped cream, sprinkle over the grated chocolate, and decorate with the whole fresh cherries.

chocolate fudge cake

SERVES 8

¾ cup butter, softened, plus extra for greasing

generous 1 cup superfine sugar

3 eggs, beaten

3 tbsp dark corn syrup

3 tbsp ground almonds

generous 1 cup self-rising flour

pinch of salt

¼ cup unsweetened cocoa

frosting

8 oz/225 g semisweet chocolate, broken into pieces

¼ cup dark brown sugar

1 cup butter, diced

5 tbsp evaporated milk

½ tsp vanilla extract

1 Grease and line the bottoms of 2 x 8-inch/20-cm round layer cake pans with parchment paper.

2 To make the frosting, place the chocolate, brown sugar, butter, evaporated milk, and vanilla extract in a heavy-bottom saucepan. Heat gently, stirring continuously, until melted. Pour into a bowl and let cool. Cover and let chill in the refrigerator for 1 hour, or until spreadable.

3 Preheat the oven to 350°F/180°C. Place the butter and superfine sugar in a bowl and beat together until light and fluffy. Gradually beat in the eggs. Stir in the corn syrup and ground almonds. Sift the flour, salt, and cocoa into a separate bowl, then fold into the cake batter. Add a little water, if necessary, to make a dropping consistency.

4 Spoon the cake batter into the prepared pans and bake in the preheated oven for 30–35 minutes, or until springy to the touch and a toothpick inserted in the center comes out clean.

5 Let stand in the pans for 5 minutes, then turn out onto wire racks to cool completely. When the cakes have cooled, sandwich them together with half the frosting. Spread the remaining frosting over the top and sides of the cake, swirling it to create a decorative appearance.

chocolate brownie cake

SERVES 10

scant 1 cup butter

4 oz/115 g semisweet chocolate, broken into pieces

1¼ cups granulated sugar

½ cup light brown sugar

4 eggs, beaten

¾ cup all-purpose flour

1 tsp vanilla extract

pinch of salt

½ cup dried cranberries

scant ½ cup toasted slivered almonds, plus extra to decorate

frosting

4 oz/115 g semisweet chocolate, broken into pieces

2 tbsp butter

2 cups confectioners' sugar

3–4 tbsp milk

1 Preheat the oven to 350°F/180°C. Grease and line the bottoms of 2 x 7-inch/18-cm round shallow cake pans with parchment paper.

2 Place the butter in a heavy-bottom saucepan and add the chocolate. Heat gently, stirring frequently, until the mixture has melted. Remove from the heat and stir until smooth. Add the sugars, stir well, then let cool for 10 minutes.

3 Gradually add the eggs to the cooled chocolate mixture, beating well after each addition. Stir in the flour, vanilla extract, and salt. Stir in the cranberries and slivered almonds, mix, then divide between the prepared cake pans.

4 Bake in the preheated oven for 25–30 minutes, or until springy to the touch. Remove from the oven and let cool slightly in the pans before turning out onto a wire rack to cool completely.

5 To make the frosting, melt the chocolate and butter in a heavy-bottom saucepan and stir until smooth. Gradually beat in the confectioners' sugar with enough milk to create a smooth spreading consistency. Use a little of the frosting to sandwich the 2 cakes together, then spread the top and sides with the remainder, swirling the top to create a decorative effect. Sprinkle with slivered almonds and let the frosting set before serving.

chocolate ganache cake

SERVES 10

¾ cup unsalted butter, plus extra for greasing

¾ cup superfine sugar

4 eggs, lightly beaten

1¾ cups self-rising flour

1 tbsp unsweetened cocoa

1¾ oz/50 g semisweet chocolate, melted

7 oz/200 g chocolate-flavored confectionery coating, to decorate

ganache

2 cups heavy cream

13 oz/375 g semisweet chocolate, broken into pieces

1 Preheat the oven to 350°F/180°C. Grease and line the bottom of an 8-inch/20-cm round springform cake pan with parchment paper.

2 Beat the butter and sugar together in a bowl until light and fluffy. Gradually add the eggs, beating well after each addition. Sift the flour and cocoa together, then fold into the cake batter. Fold in the melted chocolate. Pour into the prepared pan and smooth the top. Bake in the preheated oven for 40 minutes, or until springy to the touch. Let the cake cool for 5 minutes, then turn out onto a wire rack. Cut into 2 layers when completely cool.

3 To make the ganache, place the cream in a saucepan and bring to a boil, stirring. Add the chocolate and stir until melted. Pour into a bowl, let cool, then chill for 2 hours, or until set and firm. Beat the mixture until light and fluffy and set aside. Reserve one-third of the ganache. Use the remainder to sandwich the cake together and spread over the cake. Melt the confectionery coating and spread it over a large sheet of parchment paper. Let cool until just set. Cut into strips a little wider than the height of the cake. Place the strips around the edge of the cake, overlapping them slightly. Pipe the reserved ganache onto the top of the cake.

Step 2

Step 3

Step 3

chocolate & walnut cake

SERVES 8

4 eggs

2/3 cup superfine sugar

2 3/4 oz/75 g semisweet chocolate, broken into pieces

scant 1 cup all-purpose flour

1 tbsp unsweetened cocoa

2 tbsp butter, melted, plus extra for greasing

1 cup finely chopped walnuts, plus extra halves to decorate

frosting

2 3/4 oz/75 g semisweet chocolate, broken into pieces

1/2 cup butter

1 1/2 cups confectioners' sugar

2 tbsp milk

1 Preheat the oven to 325°F/160°C. Grease and line a 7-inch/18-cm round deep cake pan with parchment paper.

2 Place the eggs and superfine sugar in a bowl and beat with a handheld electric mixer for 10 minutes, or until foamy and a trail is left when the beaters are dragged across the surface. Melt the chocolate in a heatproof bowl set over a saucepan of gently simmering water.

3 Sift the flour and cocoa together and fold into the egg-and-sugar mixture with a spoon or a spatula. Fold in the butter, melted chocolate, and chopped walnuts. Pour into the prepared pan and bake in the preheated oven for 30–35 minutes, or until springy to the touch.

4 Let cool in the pan for 5 minutes, then transfer to a wire rack and let cool completely.

5 To make the frosting, melt the chocolate in a heatproof bowl set over a saucepan of gently simmering water and let cool slightly. Beat together the butter, confectioners' sugar, and milk until the mixture is pale and fluffy. Beat in the melted chocolate.

6 Cut the cake into 2 layers of equal thickness. Place the bottom half on a serving plate, spread with half the frosting, and put the other half on top. Smooth the remaining frosting over the top of the cake with a spatula, swirling it slightly to create a decorative effect. Decorate the cake with walnut halves and serve.

hot chocolate cheesecake

SERVES 8–10

scant 1½ cups all-purpose flour, plus extra for dusting

2 tbsp unsweetened cocoa

4 tbsp butter, plus extra for greasing

2 tbsp superfine sugar

¼ cup ground almonds

1 egg yolk

confectioners' sugar and grated chocolate, to decorate

filling

2 eggs, separated

scant ½ cup superfine sugar

1½ cups cream cheese

¼ tbsp ground almonds

⅔ cup heavy cream

¼ cup unsweetened cocoa, sifted

1 tsp vanilla extract

1 Grease an 8-inch/20-cm round loose-bottom cake pan. To make the pie dough, sift the flour and cocoa into a bowl and rub in the butter until the mixture resembles fine breadcrumbs. Stir in the sugar and ground almonds. Add the egg yolk and enough water to make a soft dough.

2 Roll the pie dough out on a lightly floured work surface and use to line the prepared pan. Let chill for 30 minutes. Preheat the oven to 325°F/160°C.

3 To make the filling, put the egg yolks and sugar in a large bowl and whisk until thick and pale. Beat in the cream cheese, ground almonds, cream, cocoa, and vanilla extract until well combined.

4 Put the egg whites in a large clean bowl and whisk until stiff but not dry. Stir a little of the egg white into the cream cheese mixture, then fold in the remainder. Pour into the pastry shell.

5 Bake in the preheated oven for 1½ hours, until well risen and just firm to the touch. Carefully remove from the pan, dust with confectioners' sugar, and sprinkle with grated chocolate. Serve warm.

deep chocolate cheesecake

SERVES 6–8

1 cup finely crushed graham crackers

2 tsp unsweetened cocoa

4 tbsp butter, melted, plus extra for greasing

chocolate leaves, to decorate

chocolate layer

1 lb 12 oz/800 g mascarpone cheese

scant 2 cups confectioners' sugar, sifted

juice of ½ orange

finely grated rind of 1 orange

6 oz/175 g semisweet chocolate, melted

2 tbsp cognac

1 Grease an 8-inch/20-cm round loose-bottom cake pan. Put the crushed graham crackers, cocoa, and melted butter into a large bowl and mix well. Press the crumb mixture evenly over the bottom of the prepared pan.

2 To make the chocolate layer, put the mascarpone cheese and confectioners' sugar into a bowl and stir in the orange juice and rind. Add the melted chocolate and cognac and mix together until thoroughly combined. Spread the chocolate mixture evenly over the crumb layer. Cover with plastic wrap and let chill in the refrigerator for at least 4 hours.

3 Remove the cheesecake from the refrigerator, turn out onto a serving plate, and decorate with chocolate leaves before serving.

mocha cheesecake

SERVES 10

6 tbsp butter, plus extra for greasing

1¾ cups crushed chocolate graham crackers

6 oz /75 g semisweet chocolate, broken into pieces

1 tbsp instant expresso dissolved in 6 tbsp boiling water

6 tbsp cold water

2 tbsp gelatin

13 oz/375 g ricotta cheese

scant ½ cup superfine sugar

1 cup heavy cream, softly whipped

unsweetened cocoa, for sprinkling

whipped cream, to serve

1 Grease an 8-inch/20-cm springform cake pan. Melt the butter in a large saucepan, then remove from the heat. Add the crushed crackers and mix well. Spoon over the bottom of the pan and press down evenly. Chill until firm.

2 Place the chocolate and expresso liquid in a heatproof bowl. Set the bowl over a saucepan of gently simmering water until melted. Cool slightly. Pour the cold water into another heatproof bowl, sprinkle the gelatin evenly over the surface, and let stand for 5 minutes, until spongy. Set the bowl over a saucepan of gently simmering water until melted. Remove from the heat.

3 Place the ricotta cheese, sugar, and chocolate mixture in a large bowl, beat together with an electric handheld mixer until smooth, then beat in the melted gelatin. Fold in the cream, then spoon over the cracker crust. Chill in the refrigerator for at least 3 hours, or until firm.

4 Sift the cocoa over the top of the cheesecake, remove the cake from the pan, and transfer to a serving plate. Serve with whipped cream.

Step 1

Step 3

Step 4

citrus mousse cake

SERVES 12

¾ cup butter, plus extra for greasing

¾ cup superfine sugar

4 eggs, lightly beaten

1¾ cups self-rising flour

1 tbsp unsweetened cocoa

1¾ oz/50 g orange-flavored semisweet chocolate, melted

peeled orange segments, to decorate

orange mousse

2 eggs, separated

¼ cup superfine sugar

¾ cup freshly squeezed orange juice

2 tsp gelatin

3 tbsp water

1¼ cups heavy cream

1 Preheat the oven to 350°F/180°C. Grease an 8-inch/20-cm round springform cake pan and line the bottom with parchment paper.

2 Beat the butter and sugar in a bowl until light and fluffy. Gradually add the eggs, beating well after each addition. Sift together the flour and cocoa, then fold into the creamed mixture. Fold in the melted chocolate.

3 Pour into the prepared pan and level the top. Bake in the preheated oven for 40 minutes, or until springy to the touch. Let cool for 5 minutes in the pan, then turn out onto a wire rack and let cool completely. Cut the cold cake into 2 layers.

4 To make the orange mousse, beat the egg yolks and sugar until pale, then whisk in the orange juice. Sprinkle the gelatin over the water in a small heatproof bowl and let it turn spongy, then place over a saucepan of hot water and stir until dissolved. Stir into the egg yolk mixture. Whip the cream until it holds its shape. Reserve a little for decoration and fold the remainder into the mixture. Whisk the egg whites until standing in soft peaks, then fold in. Let stand in a cool place until starting to set, stirring occasionally.

5 Place a cake layer back in the pan. Pour in the mousse and press the other cake layer on top. Chill until set. Transfer to a plate, then spoon teaspoonfuls of cream around the top and arrange orange segments in the center.

mega chip cookies

MAKES 12

1 cup butter, softened

scant ¾ cup superfine sugar

1 egg yolk, lightly beaten

2 tsp vanilla extract

2 cups all-purpose flour

½ cup unsweetened cocoa

pinch of salt

½ cup milk chocolate chips

½ cup white chocolate chips

4 oz/115 g semisweet chocolate, coarsely chopped

1 Preheat the oven to 375°F/190°C. Line 2–3 cookie sheets with parchment paper.

2 Put the butter and sugar into a bowl and mix well with a wooden spoon, then beat in the egg yolk and vanilla extract. Sift together the flour, cocoa, and salt into the mixture, add both kinds of chocolate chips, and stir until thoroughly combined.

3 Make 12 balls of the mixture, put them on the prepared cookie sheets, spaced well apart, and flatten slightly. Press the pieces of semisweet chocolate into the cookies.

4 Bake in the preheated oven for 12–15 minutes. Let cool on the cookie sheets for 5–10 minutes, then, using a spatula, carefully transfer to wire racks to cool completely.

chocolate cookie sandwiches

MAKES 15

1 cup butter, softened

scant 3/4 cup superfine sugar

2 tsp finely grated orange rind

1 egg yolk, lightly beaten

2 tsp vanilla extract

2 1/4 cups all-purpose flour

1/4 cup unsweetened cocoa

pinch of salt

3 1/2 oz/100 g semisweet chocolate, finely chopped

chocolate filling

1/2 cup heavy cream

7 oz/200 g white chocolate, broken into pieces

1 tsp orange extract

1 Preheat the oven to 375°F/190°C. Line 2 cookie sheets with parchment paper.

2 Put the butter, sugar, and orange rind into a bowl and mix well with a wooden spoon, then beat in the egg yolk and vanilla extract. Sift the flour, cocoa, and salt together into the mixture, add the semisweet chocolate, and stir until thoroughly combined.

3 Scoop up tablespoons of the dough, roll into balls, and put on the prepared cookie sheets, spaced well apart. Gently flatten and smooth the tops with the back of a spoon. Bake in the preheated oven for 10–15 minutes, until golden brown. Let cool on the cookie sheets for 5–10 minutes, then carefully transfer to wire racks to cool completely.

4 To make the filling, bring the cream to a boil in a small saucepan, then remove the saucepan from the heat. Stir in the white chocolate until the mixture is smooth, then stir in the orange extract. When the mixture is completely cool, use to sandwich the cookies together in pairs.

chocolate mint cookies

MAKES 15

1 cup butter, softened

scant 3/4 cup superfine sugar

1 egg yolk, lightly beaten

2 tsp vanilla extract

2 1/4 cups all-purpose flour

1/2 cup unsweetened cocoa

pinch of salt

1/3 cup candied cherries, finely chopped

15 after-dinner mint thins

chocolate coating

4 oz/115 g semisweet chocolate, broken into pieces

2 oz/55 g white chocolate, broken into pieces

1 Put the butter and sugar into a bowl and mix well with a wooden spoon, then beat in the egg yolk and vanilla extract. Sift the flour, cocoa, and salt together into the mixture, add the cherries, and stir until thoroughly combined. Halve the dough, shape into balls, wrap in plastic wrap, and chill in the refrigerator for 30–60 minutes.

2 Preheat the oven to 375°F/190°C. Line 2 cookie sheets with parchment paper. Unwrap the dough and roll out between 2 sheets of parchment paper. Stamp out cookies with a 2 1/2-inch/6-cm plain square cutter and put them on the prepared cookie sheets, spaced well apart. Bake in the preheated oven for 10–15 minutes, until firm. Immediately place an after-dinner mint on top of half the cookies, then cover with the remaining cookies. Press down gently and let cool.

3 Melt the semisweet chocolate in a heatproof bowl set over a saucepan of gently simmering water and let cool. Put the cookies on a wire rack, spoon the semisweet chocolate over them, and let set. Melt the white chocolate in a heatproof bowl set over a saucepan of barely simmering water, then let cool. Drizzle over the cookies, then let set.

Step 1

Step 2

Step 3

cappuccino cookies

MAKES 30

2 envelopes instant cappuccino powder

1 tbsp hot water

1 cup butter, softened

scant 3/4 cup superfine sugar

1 egg yolk, lightly beaten

2½ cups all-purpose flour

pinch of salt

6 oz/175 g white chocolate, broken into pieces

unsweetened cocoa, for dusting

1 Empty the cappuccino powder into a small bowl and stir in the hot, but not boiling, water to make a paste.

2 Put the butter and sugar into a bowl and mix well with a wooden spoon, then beat in the egg yolk and cappuccino paste. Sift the flour and salt into the mixture and stir until thoroughly combined. Halve the dough, wrap in plastic wrap, and chill in the refrigerator for 30–60 minutes.

3 Preheat the oven to 375°F/190°C. Line 2 cookie sheets with parchment paper.

4 Unwrap the dough and roll out between 2 sheets of parchment paper. Stamp out cookies with a 2½-inch/6-cm plain round cutter and put them on the prepared cookie sheets, spaced well apart.

5 Bake in the preheated oven for 10–12 minutes, until golden brown. Let cool on the cookie sheets for 5–10 minutes, then carefully transfer to wire racks to cool completely.

6 When the cookies are cool, put the chocolate into a heatproof bowl and set over a saucepan of gently simmering water until melted. Remove the bowl from the heat and let cool, then spoon the chocolate over the cookies. Gently tap the wire racks to level the surface and let set. Dust with cocoa.

black & white cookies

MAKES 20

½ cup unsalted butter, softened, plus extra for greasing

1 tsp vanilla extract

scant 1 cup superfine sugar

2 eggs

2⅔ cups all-purpose flour

½ tsp baking powder

scant 1 cup milk

frosting

2 cups confectioners' sugar

½ cup heavy cream

⅛ tsp vanilla extract

2¾ oz/75 g semisweet chocolate, broken into pieces

1 Preheat the oven to 375°F/190°C. Grease 3 baking sheets.

2 Put the butter, vanilla extract, and superfine sugar in a large bowl. Beat the mixture with an electric mixer until light and fluffy, then beat in the eggs one at a time.

3 Sift together the flour and baking powder and fold into the beaten mixture, gradually adding the milk, until the mixture drops easily from the spoon.

4 Drop heaping tablespoonfuls of the mixture on the prepared baking sheets, spaced well apart. Bake in the preheated oven for 15 minutes, until turning golden at the edges and light to the touch. Transfer to wire racks to cool completely.

5 To decorate, put the confectioners' sugar into a bowl and mix in half of the cream and the vanilla extract until the frosting is thick but can still be spread. Using a metal spatula, spread half of each cookie with white frosting. Melt the chocolate in a heatproof bowl set over a saucepan of gently simmering water. Remove from the heat and stir in the remaining cream. Spread the dark frosting over the uncoated cookie halves. Let set for 10 minutes before serving.

clubs & spades

MAKES 15

1 cup butter, softened

scant 3/4 cup superfine sugar

1 egg yolk, lightly beaten

2 tsp vanilla extract

2 1/2 cups all-purpose flour

pinch of salt

generous 1/2 cup semisweet chocolate chips

filling

1/4 cup butter, softened

1 tsp dark corn syrup

3/4 cup confectioners' sugar

1 tbsp unsweetened cocoa

1 Put the butter and superfine sugar into a bowl and mix well with a wooden spoon, then beat in the egg yolk and vanilla extract. Sift the flour and salt into the mixture, add the chocolate chips, and stir until thoroughly combined. Halve the dough, wrap in plastic wrap, and chill in the refrigerator for 30–60 minutes.

2 Preheat the oven to 375°F/190°C. Line 2 cookie sheets with parchment paper.

3 Unwrap the dough and roll out between 2 sheets of parchment paper. Stamp out cookies with a 2 1/2-inch/6-cm square fluted cutter and put half of them on a prepared cookie sheet, spaced well apart. Using small club- and spade-shaped cutters, stamp out the centers of the remaining cookies and remove them. Put the cookies on the other cookie sheet, spaced well apart.

4 Bake in the preheated oven for 10–15 minutes, until light golden brown. Let cool on the cookie sheets for 5–10 minutes, then carefully transfer to wire racks to cool completely.

5 To make the filling, put the butter and corn syrup into a bowl and sift in the confectioners' sugar and cocoa. Beat well until smooth. Spread the chocolate cream over the whole cookies and top with the cutout cookies.

giant chocolate chunk cookies

MAKES 12

½ cup butter, softened

scant ⅔ cup superfine sugar

scant ⅔ cup light brown sugar

2 extra-large eggs, lightly beaten

1 tsp vanilla extract

2 cups all-purpose flour

1 tsp baking soda

10½ oz/300 g chocolate chunks

1 Preheat the oven to 350°F/180°C. Line several large baking sheets with parchment paper.

2 Place the butter and sugars in a large bowl and beat together with a handheld electric mixer until pale and creamy. Beat the eggs and vanilla extract into the mixture until smooth. Sift in the flour and baking soda and beat together until well mixed. Stir in the chocolate chunks.

3 Drop 12 large spoonfuls of the batter onto the baking sheets, spacing them well apart.

4 Bake in the preheated oven for 15–20 minutes, or until set and golden brown. Let cool on the baking sheets for 2–3 minutes, then transfer the cookies to a wire rack and let cool completely.

Step 2

Step 2

Step 3

viennese fingers

MAKES 16

scant ½ cup unsalted butter, plus extra for greasing

2 tbsp superfine sugar

½ tsp vanilla extract

scant 1 cup self-rising flour

3½ oz/100 g semisweet chocolate, broken into pieces

1 Preheat the oven to 325°F/160°C. Grease 2 cookie sheets.

2 Place the butter, sugar, and vanilla extract in a bowl and cream together until pale and fluffy. Stir in the flour, mixing evenly to a fairly stiff dough.

3 Place the mixture in a pastry bag fitted with a large star tip and pipe about 16 bars, each 2½ inches/6 cm long, onto the prepared cookie sheets.

4 Bake in the preheated oven for 10–15 minutes, until pale golden. Cool for 2–3 minutes on the cookie sheets, then lift carefully onto a wire rack with a spatula to finish cooling.

5 Place the chocolate in a small heatproof bowl set over a saucepan of gently simmering water until melted. Remove from the heat. Dip the ends of each cookie into the chocolate to coat, then place on a sheet of parchment paper and let set.

lebkuchen

MAKES 60

3 eggs

1 cup superfine sugar

½ cup all-purpose flour

2 tsp unsweetened cocoa

1 tsp ground cinnamon

½ tsp ground cardamom

¼ tsp ground cloves

¼ tsp ground nutmeg

generous 1 cup ground almonds

scant ⅓ cup chopped candied peel

to decorate

4 oz/115 g semisweet chocolate, broken into pieces

4 oz/115 g white chocolate, broken into pieces

sugar crystals

1 Preheat the oven to 350°F/180°C. Line several cookie sheets with parchment paper.

2 Put the eggs and sugar in a heatproof bowl set over a saucepan of gently simmering water. Whisk until thick and foamy. Remove the bowl from the pan and continue to whisk for 2 minutes.

3 Sift the flour, cocoa, cinnamon, cardamom, cloves, and nutmeg into the bowl and stir in with the ground almonds and candied peel. Drop generous teaspoonfuls of the cookie dough onto the prepared cookie sheets, spreading them gently into smooth mounds.

4 Bake in the preheated oven for 15–20 minutes, until light brown and slightly soft to the touch. Cool on the cookie sheets for 10 minutes, then transfer to wire racks to cool completely.

5 Put the semisweet chocolate and white chocolate into 2 separate heatproof bowls set over 2 saucepans of gently simmering water until melted. Dip half the cookies in the melted semisweet chocolate and half in the white chocolate. Sprinkle with sugar crystals and let set.

sugared hearts

MAKES 30

1 cup butter, softened

1½ cups superfine sugar

1 egg yolk, lightly beaten

2 tsp vanilla extract

generous 1¾ cups all-purpose flour

¼ cup unsweetened cocoa

pinch of salt

3–4 food coloring pastes

3½ oz/100 g semisweet chocolate, broken into pieces

1 Place the butter and half the sugar in a large bowl and beat together until light and fluffy, then beat in the egg yolk and vanilla extract. Sift together the flour, cocoa, and salt into the mixture and stir until combined. Halve the dough, shape into balls, wrap in plastic wrap, and chill in the refrigerator for 30–60 minutes.

2 Preheat the oven to 375°F/190°C. Line 2 large baking sheets with parchment paper. Unwrap the dough and roll out between 2 sheets of parchment paper. Cut out cookies with a heart-shaped cutter and place them on the baking sheets, spaced well apart. Bake in the preheated oven for 10–15 minutes, or until firm. Let cool on the baking sheets for 5–10 minutes, then transfer to wire racks to cool completely.

3 Meanwhile, divide the remaining sugar among 4 small plastic bags or bowls. Add a little food coloring paste to each and rub in until well mixed. Wear a plastic glove if mixing in bowls to prevent your hands from getting stained. Melt the chocolate in a heatproof bowl set over a saucepan of gently simmering water.

4 Let the cookies cool on the racks. Spread the melted chocolate over them and sprinkle with the colored sugar. Let set.

chocolate biscotti

MAKES 24

2 tbsp unsalted butter, plus extra for greasing

6 oz/175 g semisweet chocolate, broken into pieces

2½ cups self-rising flour, plus extra for dusting

1½ tsp baking powder

scant ½ cup superfine sugar

½ cup cornmeal

finely grated rind of 1 lemon

2 tsp amaretto

1 egg, lightly beaten

¾ cup coarsely chopped pistachios

2 tbsp confectioners' sugar, for dusting

1 Preheat the oven to 325°F/160°C. Grease a cookie sheet. Put the butter and chocolate in a heatproof bowl set over a saucepan of gently simmering water. Stir over low heat until melted and smooth. Remove from the heat and let cool slightly.

2 Sift the flour and baking powder into a bowl and mix in the superfine sugar, cornmeal, lemon rind, amaretto, egg, and pistachios. Stir in the chocolate mixture and mix to a soft dough.

3 Lightly dust your hands with flour, divide the dough in half, and shape each piece into an 11-inch/28-cm long cylinder. Transfer the cylinders to the prepared cookie sheet and flatten with the palm of your hand to about ¾ inch/2 cm thick. Bake in the preheated oven for about 20 minutes, until firm to the touch.

4 Remove the cookie sheet from the oven and let the cylinders cool. Do not turn the oven off. When cool, put the cylinders on a cutting board and slice them diagonally into thin cookies. Return them to the cookie sheet and bake for an additional 10 minutes, until crisp. Remove from the oven and transfer to a wire rack to cool. Dust lightly with confectioners' sugar.

VARIATION

Instead of pistachios, use ¾ cup of almonds, coarsely chopped, and replace the amaretto with 1 tsp of vanilla extract.

2

Sensational Slices & Small Cakes

chocolate fudge brownies

MAKES 16

scant 1 cup cream cheese

½ tsp vanilla extract

generous 1 cup superfine sugar

2 eggs

6 tbsp butter, plus extra for greasing

3 tbsp unsweetened cocoa

¾ cup self-rising flour, sifted

⅓ cup chopped pecans, plus extra pecan halves to decorate

frosting

4 tbsp butter

1 tbsp milk

⅔ cup confectioners' sugar

2 tbsp unsweetened cocoa

1 Preheat the oven to 350°F/180°C. Grease an 8-inch/20-cm square shallow cake pan and line the bottom with parchment paper.

2 Beat together the cream cheese, vanilla extract, and 5 teaspoons of the superfine sugar until smooth, then set aside.

3 Beat together the eggs and the remaining superfine sugar until light and fluffy. Place the butter and cocoa in a small saucepan and heat gently, stirring until the butter melts and the mixture combines, then stir it into the egg mixture. Fold in the flour and chopped pecans.

4 Pour half of the cake batter into the prepared pan and smooth the top. Carefully spread the cream cheese mixture over it, then cover it with the remaining cake batter. Bake in the preheated oven for 40–45 minutes. Let cool in the pan.

5 To make the frosting, melt the butter in a small saucepan with the milk. Stir in the confectioners' sugar and cocoa. Spread the frosting over the brownies and decorate with pecan halves. Let the frosting set, then cut into squares to serve.

double chocolate brownies

MAKES 9

½ cup butter, plus extra for greasing

4 oz/115 g semisweet chocolate, broken into pieces

1⅓ cups superfine sugar

pinch of salt

1 tsp vanilla extract

2 eggs

1 cup all-purpose flour

2 tbsp unsweetened cocoa

½ cup white chocolate chips

fudge sauce

4 tbsp butter

generous 1 cup superfine sugar

⅔ cup milk

generous 1 cup heavy cream

⅔ cup dark corn syrup

7 oz/200 g semisweet chocolate, broken into pieces

1 Preheat the oven to 350°F/180°C. Grease a 7-inch/18-cm square cake pan and line the bottom with parchment paper.

2 Place the butter and chocolate in a small heatproof bowl set over a saucepan of gently simmering water until melted. Stir until smooth. Let cool slightly. Stir in the sugar, salt, and vanilla extract. Add the eggs, one at a time, stirring well, until blended.

3 Sift the flour and cocoa into the cake batter and beat until smooth. Stir in the chocolate chips, then pour the batter into the prepared pan. Bake in the preheated oven for 35–40 minutes, or until the top is evenly colored and a toothpick inserted into the center comes out almost clean. Let cool slightly while you prepare the sauce.

4 To make the sauce, place the butter, sugar, milk, cream, and corn syrup in a small saucepan and heat gently until the sugar has dissolved. Bring to a boil and stir for 10 minutes, or until the mixture is a caramel color. Remove from the heat and add the chocolate. Stir until smooth. Cut the brownies into squares and serve immediately with the sauce.

chocolate crispy bites

MAKES 16

white layer

4 tbsp butter, plus extra for greasing

1 tbsp dark corn syrup

5½ oz/150 g white chocolate, broken into pieces

2 cups toasted rice cereal

dark layer

4 tbsp butter

2 tbsp dark corn syrup

4½ oz/125 g semisweet chocolate, broken into pieces

3 cups toasted rice cereal

1 Grease an 8-inch/20-cm square cake pan and line with parchment paper.

2 To make the white layer, melt the butter, corn syrup, and chocolate in a heatproof bowl set over a saucepan of gently simmering water. Remove from the heat and stir in the rice cereal until it is well combined. Press into the prepared pan and smooth the surface. Let chill in the refrigerator.

3 To make the dark layer, melt the butter, corn syrup, and semisweet chocolate in a separate heatproof bowl set over a saucepan of gently simmering water. Remove from the heat and stir in the rice cereal. Pour over the hardened white chocolate layer and let cool, then let chill until hardened.

4 Turn out of the cake pan and cut into small squares using a sharp knife.

double chocolate pecan blondies

MAKES 12

9 oz/250 g white chocolate

3 tbsp butter, plus extra for greasing

6 oz/175 g semisweet chocolate

2 extra-large eggs

scant ½ cup superfine sugar

scant 1 cup self-rising flour

generous ¾ cup coarsely chopped pecans

1 Preheat the oven to 350°F/180°C. Grease a shallow 8-inch/20-cm square cake pan and line with parchment paper.

2 Break up 3 oz/85 g of the white chocolate and place in a heatproof bowl, then add the butter. Set the bowl over a saucepan of gently simmering water and heat, stirring occasionally, until melted and smooth. Meanwhile, coarsely chop the remaining white chocolate and the semisweet chocolate.

3 Beat the eggs and sugar together in a large bowl, then stir in the melted chocolate mixture. Sift the flour over the top. Add the chopped chocolate and pecans. Mix well.

4 Spoon the batter into the prepared pan and level the surface. Bake in the preheated oven for 35–40 minutes, or until golden brown and just firm to the touch in the center. Let stand in the pan until completely cooled and the chocolate chunks inside have set, then turn out and cut into pieces.

Step 2

Step 3

Step 4

chocolate chip shortbread

MAKES 8

generous ¾ cup all-purpose flour

scant ½ cup cornstarch

generous ¼ cup superfine sugar

½ cup butter, diced, plus extra for greasing

¼ cup semisweet chocolate chips

1 Preheat the oven to 325°F/160°C. Grease a 9-inch/23-cm loose-bottom fluted tart pan.

2 Sift the flour and cornstarch into a large bowl. Stir in the sugar, then add the butter and rub it in until the mixture starts to bind together.

3 Transfer to the prepared tart pan and press evenly over the bottom. Prick the surface with a fork. Sprinkle with the chocolate chips and press lightly into the surface.

4 Bake in the preheated oven for 35–40 minutes, or until cooked but not browned. Mark into 8 portions with a sharp knife. Let cool in the pan for 10 minutes, then transfer to a wire rack to cool completely. Once cool, cut into 8 pieces.

caramel chocolate shortbread

MAKES 12

½ cup unsalted butter, plus extra for greasing

scant 1¼ cups all-purpose flour

¼ cup superfine sugar

filling & topping

scant 1 cup butter

generous ½ cup superfine sugar

3 tbsp dark corn syrup

14 oz/400 g canned sweetened condensed milk

7 oz/200 g semisweet chocolate, broken into pieces

1 Preheat the oven to 350°F/180°C. Grease a 9-inch/23-cm square shallow cake pan and line the bottom with parchment paper.

2 Place the butter, flour, and sugar in a food processor and process until they begin to bind together. Press the mixture into the prepared pan and smooth the top. Bake in the preheated oven for 20–25 minutes, or until golden.

3 Meanwhile, make the filling. Place the butter, sugar, corn syrup, and condensed milk in a saucepan and heat gently until the sugar has dissolved. Bring to a boil and simmer for 6–8 minutes, stirring continuously, until the mixture becomes thick. Remove the shortbread from the oven, then pour over the filling and chill in the refrigerator until firm.

4 To make the topping, melt the chocolate in a heatproof bowl set over a saucepan of gently simmering water. Remove from the heat and let cool slightly, then spread over the filling. Chill in the refrigerator until set. Cut into 12 pieces with a sharp knife to serve.

chocolate peanut butter squares

MAKES 20

10½ oz/300 g milk chocolate

2½ cups all-purpose flour

1 tsp baking powder

1 cup butter

1¾ cups light brown sugar

2 cups rolled oats

½ cup chopped mixed nuts

1 egg, beaten

14 oz/400 g canned sweetened condensed milk

⅓ cup chunky peanut butter

1 Preheat the oven to 350°F/180°C. Grease a 12 x 8-inch/30 x 20-cm cake pan and line the bottom with parchment paper.

2 Finely chop the chocolate. Sift the flour and baking powder into a large bowl. Add the butter to the flour mixture and rub in using your fingertips until the mixture resembles breadcrumbs. Stir in the sugar, rolled oats, and chopped nuts.

3 Put one-quarter of the mixture into a bowl and stir in the chocolate. Set aside.

4 Stir the egg into the remaining mixture, then press into the bottom of the prepared cake pan. Bake in the preheated oven for 15 minutes.

5 Meanwhile, mix the condensed milk and peanut butter together. Pour onto the cooked mixture in the cake pan and spread evenly, then sprinkle the reserved chocolate mixture on top and press down lightly.

6 Return to the oven and bake for an additional 20 minutes, until golden brown. Let cool in the pan, then cut into squares.

chocolate peppermint bars

MAKES 16

½ cup unsalted butter, plus extra for greasing

½ cup superfine sugar

generous 1⅓ cups all-purpose flour

filling & topping

2½ cups confectioners' sugar

2–4 tbsp warm water

1 tsp peppermint extract

a few drops of green edible food coloring (optional)

6 oz/175 g semisweet chocolate, broken into pieces

1 Preheat the oven to 350°F/180°C. Grease a 12 x 8-inch/30 x 20-cm jelly roll pan and line with parchment paper.

2 Beat the butter and superfine sugar together until pale and fluffy. Stir in the flour until the mixture binds together.

3 Knead the mixture to form a smooth dough, then press into the prepared pan. Prick the surface all over with a fork. Bake in the preheated oven for 10–15 minutes, or until lightly browned and just firm to the touch. Remove from the oven and let cool in the pan.

4 To make the filling, sift the confectioners' sugar into a bowl. Gradually add the water, then add the peppermint extract and the food coloring, if using. Spread the filling over the bottom, then let set.

5 Melt the chocolate in a heatproof bowl set over a saucepan of gently simmering water, then remove from the heat and spread it over the filling. Let set, then cut into slices.

Step 2

Step 4

Step 5

chocolate chip bars

MAKES 9

½ cup unsalted butter, plus extra for greasing

⅓ cup superfine sugar

1 tbsp dark corn syrup

4 cups rolled oats

½ cup semisweet chocolate chips

⅓ cup golden raisins

1 Preheat the oven to 350°F/180°C. Grease an 8-inch/20-cm square shallow cake pan.

2 Place the butter, sugar, and corn syrup in a saucepan and cook over low heat, stirring continuously, until the butter has melted and the mixture is well combined.

3 Remove the pan from the heat and stir in the rolled oats until they are well coated. Add the chocolate chips and the golden raisins and mix well to combine.

4 Transfer to the prepared pan and press down well. Bake in the preheated oven for 30 minutes. Let cool slightly, then gently use a knife to mark into bars. When almost cooled, cut into bars or squares and transfer to a wire rack to cool completely.

rocky road pieces

MAKES 18

4½ oz/125 g milk chocolate

1 cup mini marshmallows

¼ cup chopped walnuts

8 plumped dried apricots, chopped

1 Line a cookie sheet with parchment paper. Break the chocolate into small pieces and place in a large heatproof bowl. Set the bowl over a saucepan of simmering water and stir until the chocolate has melted.

2 Stir in the marshmallows, walnuts, and apricots, until well coated.

3 Place heaping teaspoons of the marshmallow mixture onto the prepared cookie sheet, then let chill in the refrigerator until set.

chocolate slabs

MAKES 12

scant 1 cup butter, plus extra for greasing

3½ oz/100 g semisweet chocolate, broken into pieces

⅓ cup water

2½ cups all-purpose flour

2 tsp baking powder

1⅓ cups light brown sugar

⅓ cup sour cream

2 eggs, beaten

frosting

7 oz/200 g semisweet chocolate, broken into pieces

6 tbsp water

3 tbsp light cream

1 tbsp butter, chilled

1 Preheat the oven to 375°F/190°C. Grease a 9-inch/23-cm square cake pan and line the bottom with parchment paper.

2 Melt the butter and chocolate with the water in a saucepan over low heat, stirring frequently. Sift the flour and baking powder into a mixing bowl and stir in the sugar. Pour the chocolate mixture into the bowl and then beat well until all of the ingredients are evenly mixed. Stir in the sour cream, followed by the eggs.

3 Pour the cake batter into the prepared pan and bake in the preheated oven for 40–45 minutes, until springy to the touch.

4 Let the cake cool slightly in the pan before turning it out onto a wire rack. Let cool completely.

5 To make the frosting, melt the chocolate with the water in a saucepan over very low heat, stir in the cream, and remove from the heat. Stir in the butter, then pour the frosting over the cooled cake, using a spatula to spread it evenly over the top of the cake. Cut into squares to serve.

pear & chocolate squares

MAKES 16

generous 1 cup whole wheat flour

generous 1 cup white self-rising flour

¾ cup butter, cut into small pieces, plus extra for greasing

1 cup ground almonds

generous ⅓ cup superfine sugar

2¾ cups firm ripe pears, peeled, cored, and coarsely chopped (about 1 lb/450 g)

2 extra-large eggs

⅓ cup unsweetened cocoa

2 tsp baking powder

scant 1 cup dark brown sugar

5 tbsp milk

1 Preheat the oven to 350°F/180°C. Grease a deep 7-inch/18-cm square cake pan and line with parchment paper. Sift the whole wheat flour and self-rising flour into a bowl. Add the butter and rub in with your fingertips until the mixture resembles fine breadcrumbs.

2 Transfer 4 heaping tablespoons of the mixture to a separate bowl. Add the ground almonds, superfine sugar, pears, and the white of one egg. Mix well.

3 Sift the unsweetened cocoa and baking powder together. Stir into the remaining rubbed-in mixture with the brown sugar. Add the remaining egg white, both egg yolks, and milk. Mix well.

4 Spread half of the chocolate mixture over the bottom of the prepared cake pan—it doesn't need to be even. Spread the pear mixture over the top. Cover with the remaining chocolate mixture and level the surface. Bake for 1 hour 10 minutes–1 hour 20 minutes, or until risen and the center is firm to the touch. Let cool in the pan, then turn out and cut into squares.

Step 1

Step 2

Step 4

chocolate refrigerator slices

SERVES 10–12

2 tbsp dark rum or orange juice

1/3 cup raisins

6 tbsp unsalted butter

3 tbsp dark corn syrup

6 oz/175 g semisweet chocolate, broken into pieces

2 cups lightly crushed graham crackers

1/3 cup candied cherries, halved

1/2 cup macadamia nuts, coarsely chopped

grated rind of 1 orange

topping

2 oz/55 g semisweet chocolate, broken into pieces

2 tbsp unsalted butter

1 oz/25 g white chocolate, broken into pieces

1 Put the rum and raisins in a bowl and let soak for several hours, or preferably overnight. Line an 8 x 4 x 2-inch/ 20 x 10 x 5-cm loaf pan with plastic wrap.

2 Put the butter, corn syrup, and semisweet chocolate in a saucepan and heat gently until the chocolate has melted. Remove from the heat and stir in the raisins, graham crackers, candied cherries, macadamia nuts, and orange rind.

3 Transfer the mixture to the prepared pan. Let chill until firm. Turn the cake out onto a serving plate and remove the plastic wrap.

4 To make the topping, put the semisweet chocolate and butter in a heatproof bowl set over a saucepan of gently simmering water and heat until melted. Stir until smooth, then spread over the top and sides of the cake. In a separate heatproof bowl, melt the white chocolate and drizzle over the top of the cake. Let chill until the topping has set. Serve cut into thin slices.

chocolate butterfly cakes

MAKES 12

½ cup butter

½ cup superfine sugar

1¼ cups self-rising flour

2 eggs

2 tbsp unsweetened cocoa

1 oz/25 g semisweet chocolate, melted

confectioners' sugar, for dusting

lemon buttercream

6 tbsp butter, softened

1⅓ cups confectioners' sugar, sifted

grated rind of ½ lemon

1 tbsp lemon juice

1 Preheat the oven to 350°F/180°C. Place 12 baking cups in a shallow muffin pan.

2 Place the butter, superfine sugar, flour, eggs, and cocoa in a large bowl and beat with a handheld electric mixer until the mixture is just smooth. Beat in the melted chocolate.

3 Spoon the batter into the baking cups. Bake in the preheated oven for 15 minutes, or until springy to the touch. Transfer to a wire rack and let cool.

4 Meanwhile, make the lemon buttercream. Place the butter in a mixing bowl and beat until fluffy, then gradually beat in the confectioners' sugar. Beat in the lemon rind and gradually add the lemon juice, beating well.

5 Cut the tops off the cakes using a serrated knife. Cut each cake top in half. Spread or pipe the buttercream over the cut surface of each cake and push the 2 cut pieces of cake top into the buttercream to form wings. Dust with confectioners' sugar.

devil's food cupcakes with chocolate frosting

MAKES 18

3½ tbsp soft margarine

½ cup dark brown sugar

2 extra-large eggs

¾ cup all-purpose flour

½ tsp baking soda

¼ cup unsweetened cocoa

½ cup sour cream

chocolate curls, to decorate

frosting

4½ oz/125 g semisweet chocolate

2 tbsp superfine sugar

⅔ cup sour cream

1 Preheat the oven to 350°F/180°C. Put 18 baking cups in a shallow muffin pan, or put 18 double-layer baking cups on a baking sheet.

2 Put the margarine, brown sugar, eggs, flour, baking soda, and cocoa in a large bowl and, using a handheld electric mixer, beat together until just smooth. Using a metal spoon, fold in the sour cream. Spoon the batter into the baking cups.

3 Bake in the preheated oven for 20 minutes, or until well risen and firm to the touch. Transfer to a wire rack to cool.

4 To make the frosting, break the chocolate into a heatproof bowl. Set the bowl over a saucepan of gently simmering water and heat until melted, stirring occasionally. Remove from the heat and let cool slightly, then whisk in the superfine sugar and sour cream until combined.

5 Spread the frosting over the tops of the cupcakes and let set in the refrigerator before serving. Serve decorated with chocolate curls.

chocolate cupcakes with gooey centers

MAKES 9

¾ cup soft margarine

generous ¾ cup superfine sugar

3 extra-large eggs

2 cups self-rising flour

3 tbsp unsweetened cocoa

6 oz/175 g semisweet chocolate

confectioners' sugar, for dusting

1 Preheat the oven to 375°F/190°C. Put 9 baking cups into a shallow muffin pan.

2 Put the margarine, superfine sugar, egg, flour, and cocoa in a large bowl and, using a handheld electric mixer, beat together until just smooth.

3 Spoon half of the batter into the baking cups. Using a teaspoon, make an indentation in the center of each cake. Cut the chocolate evenly into 9 squares and place a piece in each indentation, then spoon the remaining cake batter on top.

4 Bake the cupcakes in the preheated oven for 20 minutes, or until well risen and springy to the touch. Let the cupcakes cool for 2–3 minutes before serving warm, dusted with confectioners' sugar.

Step 1

Step 2

Step 3

chocolate scones

MAKES 9

2 cups self-rising flour, plus extra for dusting

5 tbsp unsalted butter, plus extra for greasing

1 tbsp superfine sugar

⅓ cup chocolate chips

about ⅔ cup milk, plus extra for brushing

1 Preheat the oven to 425°F/220°C. Grease a baking sheet.

2 Sift the flour into a mixing bowl. Cut the butter into small pieces and rub it into the flour with your fingertips until the mixture resembles fine breadcrumbs.

3 Stir in the sugar and chocolate chips, then mix in enough of the milk to form a soft dough.

4 On a lightly floured surface, roll out the dough to form a 4 x 6-inch/10 x 15-cm rectangle, about 1 inch/2.5 cm thick. Cut the dough into 9 squares.

5 Place the scones on the prepared baking sheet, spaced well apart. Brush the tops with a little milk and bake in the preheated oven for 10–12 minutes, until risen and golden. Cool on a wire rack.

double chocolate muffins

MAKES 12

scant ½ cup butter, softened

scant ¾ cup superfine sugar

½ cup dark brown sugar

2 eggs

⅔ cup sour cream

5 tbsp milk

2 cups all-purpose flour

1 tsp baking soda

2 tbsp unsweetened cocoa

1 cup semisweet chocolate chips

1 Preheat the oven to 375°F/190°C. Place 12 baking cups in a muffin pan.

2 Put the butter, superfine sugar, and brown sugar into a bowl and beat well. Beat in the eggs, sour cream, and milk until thoroughly mixed. Sift the flour, baking soda, and cocoa into a separate bowl and stir into the mixture. Add the chocolate chips and mix well.

3 Spoon the batter into the baking cups. Bake in the preheated oven for 25–30 minutes. Remove from the oven and let cool for 10 minutes. Transfer onto a wire rack and let cool completely.

marbled chocolate muffins

MAKES 12

2 cups all-purpose flour

1 tbsp baking powder

⅛ tsp salt

generous ½ cup superfine sugar

2 eggs

1 cup milk

6 tbsp sunflower oil or melted, cooled butter, plus extra for greasing (optional)

1 tsp vanilla extract

2 tbsp unsweetened cocoa

1 Preheat the oven to 400°F/200°C. Grease a 12-cup muffin pan or line with 12 baking cups.

2 Sift together the flour, baking powder, and salt into a large bowl. Stir in the sugar.

3 Lightly beat the eggs in a large pitcher or bowl, then beat in the milk, oil, and vanilla extract. Make a well in the center of the dry ingredients and pour in the beaten liquid ingredients. Stir gently until just combined; do not overmix.

4 Divide the batter between 2 bowls. Sift the cocoa into one of the bowls and mix until just combined. Using teaspoons, spoon the batters into the prepared muffin pan, alternating the chocolate batter and the plain batter.

5 Bake in the preheated oven for about 20 minutes, until well risen, golden brown, and firm to the touch. Let the muffins cool in the pan for 5 minutes, then serve warm or transfer to a wire rack and let cool completely.

frosted chocolate orange muffins

MAKES 12

2 oranges

about ½ cup milk

1⅔ cups all-purpose flour

½ cup unsweetened cocoa

1 tbsp baking powder

pinch of salt

generous ½ cup light brown sugar

scant 1 cup semisweet chocolate chips

2 eggs

6 tbsp sunflower oil or butter, melted and cooled, plus extra for greasing

strips of orange zest, for decorating

frosting

2 oz/55 g semisweet chocolate, broken into pieces

2 tbsp butter

2 tbsp water

1½ cups confectioners' sugar

1 Preheat the oven to 400°F/200°C. Grease a 12-cup muffin pan or line with 12 baking cups. Finely grate the rind from the oranges and squeeze the juice. Add enough milk to make up the juice to a generous 1 cup, then add the orange rind. Sift together the flour, cocoa, baking powder, and salt into a large bowl. Stir in the brown sugar and chocolate chips. Place the eggs in a large pitcher or bowl and beat lightly, then beat in the milk-and-orange mixture and the oil. Make a well in the center of the dry ingredients and pour in the beaten liquid ingredients. Stir gently until just combined but do not overmix. Spoon the batter into the prepared muffin pan.

2 Bake in the preheated oven for 20 minutes, or until well risen and firm to the touch. Let cool in the pan for 5 minutes, then transfer to a wire rack to cool completely.

3 To make the frosting, place the chocolate in a heatproof bowl, add the butter and water, then set the bowl over a saucepan of gently simmering water and heat, stirring, until melted. Remove from the heat, sift in the confectioners' sugar, and beat until smooth, then spread the frosting on top of the muffins and decorate with strips of orange zest.

Step 1

Step 1

Step 3

rocky road chocolate muffins

MAKES 12

generous 1½ cups all-purpose flour

½ cup unsweetened cocoa

1 tbsp baking powder

⅛ tsp salt

generous ½ cup superfine sugar

generous ½ cup white chocolate chips

½ cup white mini marshmallows, cut in half

2 eggs

1 cup milk

6 tbsp sunflower oil or melted, cooled butter, plus extra for greasing

1 Preheat the oven to 400°F/200°C. Grease a 12-cup muffin pan or line with 12 baking cups.

2 Sift together the flour, cocoa, baking powder, and salt into a large bowl. Stir in the sugar, chocolate chips, and marshmallows.

3 Lightly beat the eggs in a large pitcher or bowl, then beat in the milk and oil. Make a well in the center of the dry ingredients and pour in the beaten liquid ingredients. Stir gently until just combined; do not overmix.

4 Spoon the batter into the prepared muffin pan. Bake in the preheated oven for about 20 minutes, until risen and firm to the touch.

5 Let the muffins cool in the pan for 5 minutes, then serve warm or transfer to a wire rack and let cool completely.

chocolate meringues

MAKES 8

4 egg whites

1 cup superfine sugar

1 tsp cornstarch

1½ oz/40 g semisweet chocolate, grated

filling

3½ oz/100 g semisweet chocolate, broken into pieces

⅔ cup heavy cream

1 tbsp confectioners' sugar

1 tbsp cognac (optional)

1 Preheat the oven to 275°F/140°C. Line 2 cookie sheets with parchment paper.

2 Whisk the egg whites in a grease-free bowl until soft peaks form, then gradually whisk in half of the superfine sugar. Continue whisking until the mixture is very stiff and glossy.

3 Carefully fold in the remaining sugar, the cornstarch, and grated chocolate with a metal spoon or spatula. Spoon the mixture into a pastry bag fitted with a large star or plain tip. Pipe 16 large rosettes or mounds onto the prepared cookie sheets.

4 Bake in the preheated oven for about 1 hour, changing the position of the cookie sheets after 30 minutes. After about 1 hour, without opening the oven door, turn off the oven and let the meringues cool in the oven. Once cold, carefully peel off the parchment paper.

5 To make the filling, melt the chocolate in a heatproof bowl set over a saucepan of gently simmering water and carefully spread it over the bottom of the meringues. Stand them upside down on a wire rack until the chocolate has set. Whip the cream, confectioners' sugar, and cognac, if using, until the cream holds its shape, then use to sandwich the chocolate-coated meringues together in pairs.

chocolate & coconut-coated cake squares

MAKES 16

oil or melted butter, for greasing

1½ cups all-purpose flour

1 tbsp baking powder

¾ cup unsalted butter, softened

generous ¾ cup superfine sugar

3 eggs, beaten

1 tsp vanilla extract

2 tbsp milk

2 tbsp dry unsweetened coconut

icing & coating

4½ cups confectioners' sugar

⅓ cup unsweetened cocoa

⅓ cup boiling water

5 tbsp unsalted butter, melted

3 cups dry unsweetened coconut

1 Preheat the oven to 350°F/180°C. Grease and line a 9-inch/23-cm square cake pan with parchment paper.

2 Sift the flour and baking powder into a large bowl and add the butter, superfine sugar, eggs, and vanilla extract. Beat well until the batter is smooth, then stir in the milk and coconut.

3 Spoon the batter into the prepared pan and smooth the surface with a spatula. Bake in the preheated oven for 30–35 minutes, or until risen, firm, and golden brown.

4 Let cool in the pan for 10 minutes, then turn out and finish cooling on a wire rack. When the cake is cold, cut into 16 squares with a sharp knife.

5 For the icing, sift the confectioners' sugar and cocoa into a bowl. Add the water and butter and stir until smooth. Spread out the coconut on a large plate. Dip each piece of cake into the icing, holding with 2 forks to coat evenly, then toss in coconut to cover. Place on a sheet of parchment paper and let set.

chocolate madeleines

MAKES 30

3 eggs

1 egg yolk

1 tsp vanilla extract

¾ cup superfine sugar

1 cup all-purpose flour

¼ cup unsweetened cocoa

1 tsp baking powder

⅔ cup unsalted butter, melted and cooled, plus extra for greasing

confectioners' sugar, for dusting

1 Preheat the oven to 375°F/190°C. Lightly grease 30 cups in 2–3 standard-size madeleine pans.

2 Place the eggs, egg yolk, vanilla extract, and superfine sugar in a large bowl and beat with an electric handheld mixer until very pale and thick.

3 Sift in the flour, cocoa, and baking powder and fold in lightly and evenly using a metal spoon. Fold in the melted butter evenly.

4 Spoon the batter into the prepared pans, filling to about three-quarters full. Bake in the preheated oven for 8–10 minutes, until risen and springy to the touch.

5 Remove the cakes carefully from the pans and cool on a wire rack. Lightly dust with confectioners' sugar before serving. They are best eaten on the day they are made.

VARIATION

For chocolate-dipped madeleines, place 8 oz/225 g of semisweet or milk chocolate, broken into pieces, in a heatproof bowl and set the bowl over a saucepan of gently simmering water. Heat until the chocolate has melted, then dip the madeleines in the melted chocolate and place on a lined baking sheet to set.

3

Indulgent Desserts

molten chocolate puddings

SERVES 4

scant 1 cup butter, plus extra for greasing

3½ oz/100 g semisweet chocolate, broken into pieces

2 extra-large eggs

1 tsp vanilla extract

½ cup superfine sugar, plus extra for sprinkling

2 tbsp all-purpose flour

confectioners' sugar, for dusting

lightly whipped cream, to serve

1 Preheat the oven to 400°F/200°C. Grease 4 x ¾-cup ovenproof dishes or ramekins and sprinkle with superfine sugar.

2 Place the butter and chocolate in a heatproof bowl set over a saucepan of gently simmering water until melted. Stir until smooth. Let cool.

3 Place the eggs, vanilla extract, superfine sugar, and flour in a bowl and beat together. Stir in the melted chocolate mixture. Pour into the prepared dishes and place on a baking sheet. Bake in the preheated oven for 12–15 minutes, or until well risen and set on the outside but still molten inside.

4 Let stand for 1 minute, then turn out onto serving plates. Dust with confectioners' sugar and serve immediately with whipped cream.

mississippi mud pie

SERVES 12–14

crumb crust

20 graham crackers

½ cup pecans, finely chopped

1 tbsp light brown sugar

½ tsp ground cinnamon

6 tbsp butter, melted

filling

1 cup butter or margarine, plus extra for greasing

6 oz/175 g semisweet chocolate, chopped

½ cup dark corn syrup

4 extra-large eggs, beaten

½ cup pecans, finely chopped

1 Preheat the oven to 350°F/180°C. Grease a 9-inch/23-cm round springform or loose-bottom cake pan.

2 To make the crumb crust, put the graham crackers, pecans, sugar, and cinnamon into a food processor and process until fine crumbs form—do not overprocess to a powder. Add the melted butter and process again until moistened.

3 Put the crumb mixture into the prepared cake pan and press over the bottom and about 1½ inches/4 cm up the sides of the pan. Cover the pan and let chill while you make the filling.

4 To make the filling, put the butter, chocolate, and corn syrup into a saucepan over low heat and stir until melted and blended. Let cool, then beat in the eggs and pecans.

5 Pour the filling into the chilled crumb crust and smooth the surface. Bake in the preheated oven for 30 minutes, or until just set but still soft in the center. Let cool on a wire rack. Serve at room temperature or chilled.

chocolate soufflé

SERVES 4

1¼ cups milk

2 tbsp butter, plus extra for greasing

4 extra-large eggs, separated

1 tbsp cornstarch

4 tbsp superfine sugar, plus extra for sprinkling

3½ oz/100 g semisweet chocolate, broken into pieces

½ tsp vanilla extract

⅔ cup semisweet chocolate chips

confectioners' sugar, for dusting

chocolate sauce

2 tbsp cornstarch

1 tbsp superfine sugar

scant 2 cups milk

1¾ oz/50 g semisweet chocolate, broken into pieces

1 Preheat the oven to 350°F/180°C. Grease a 5-cup soufflé dish and sprinkle with superfine sugar.

2 Heat the milk with the butter in a saucepan until almost boiling. Mix the egg yolks, cornstarch, and superfine sugar in a bowl and pour in some of the hot milk mixture, whisking as you pour. Pour the cornstarch mixture into the pan with the hot milk and cook gently, stirring continuously until thickened. Add the chocolate and stir until melted. Remove from the heat and stir in the vanilla extract.

3 Whisk the egg whites until soft peaks form. Fold half the egg whites into the chocolate mixture. Fold in the remainder along with the chocolate chips. Pour into the prepared dish and bake in the preheated oven for 40–45 minutes, until well risen.

4 Meanwhile, make the sauce. Put the cornstarch and sugar in a small bowl and mix to a smooth paste with a little of the milk. Heat the remaining milk in a saucepan until almost boiling. Pour a little of the hot milk onto the cornstarch paste, mix well, then pour the cornstarch mixture into the pan with the hot milk. Cook gently, stirring until thickened. Add the chocolate to the sauce, stirring until melted. Dust the soufflé with confectioners' sugar and serve immediately with the sauce.

rich chocolate tarts

SERVES 8

1⅔ cups all-purpose flour, plus extra for dusting

½ cup butter, diced

2 tbsp confectioners' sugar

1 egg yolk

2–3 tbsp cold water

filling

9 oz/250 g semisweet chocolate, broken into pieces, plus extra, grated, for decorating

½ cup butter

½ cup confectioners' sugar

1¼ cups heavy cream

1 Place the flour in a large bowl. Add the butter and rub it in with your fingertips until the mixture resembles breadcrumbs. Add the confectioners' sugar, egg yolk, and enough water to form a soft dough. Cover and chill in the refrigerator for 15 minutes. Roll the dough out on a lightly floured surface and use to line 8 x 4-inch/10-cm shallow tart pans. Chill for 30 minutes.

2 Preheat the oven to 400°F/ 200°C. Prick the bottom of the shells with a fork and line with a little crumpled foil. Bake in the preheated oven for 10 minutes, then remove the foil and bake for 5–10 minutes, until crisp. Transfer to a wire rack to cool. Reduce the oven temperature to 325°F/160°C.

3 To make the filling, place the chocolate, butter, and confectioners' sugar in a heatproof bowl set over a saucepan of simmering water and heat until melted. Remove from the heat and stir in a generous ¾ cup heavy cream. Remove the shells from the pans and place on a baking sheet. Fill each shell with the chocolate. Bake for 5 minutes. Cool, then chill until required. To serve, whip the remaining cream and pipe or spoon into the center of each tart. Decorate with grated chocolate.

Step 1

Step 1

Step 3

lemon & chocolate tart

SERVES 8

¾ cup all-purpose flour

¼ cup unsweetened cocoa

5½ tbsp butter

¼ cup ground almonds

¼ cup superfine sugar

1 egg, beaten

chocolate curls, to decorate

filling

4 eggs

1 egg yolk

1 cup superfine sugar

⅔ cup heavy cream

grated rind and juice of 2 lemons

1 Sift the flour and cocoa into a food processor. Add the butter, ground almonds, sugar, and egg and process until the mixture forms a ball. Gather the dough together and press into a flattened ball. Place in the center of an 8-inch/20-cm round loose-bottom tart pan and press evenly over the bottom of the pan with your fingers, then work the pie dough up the sides with your thumbs. Let any excess dough go over the edge. Cover and let chill for 30 minutes.

2 Preheat the oven to 400°F/200°C. Trim off any excess dough. Prick the bottom of the dough lightly with a fork, then line with parchment paper and fill with dried beans. Bake in the preheated oven for 12–15 minutes, or until the dough no longer looks raw. Remove the beans and paper, return to the oven, and bake for an additional 10 minutes, or until the pastry is firm. Let cool. Reduce the oven temperature to 300°F/150°C.

3 To make the filling, whisk the whole eggs, egg yolk, and sugar together until smooth. Add the cream and whisk again, then stir in the lemon rind and juice. Pour the filling into the pastry shell and bake for 50 minutes, or until just set. When the tart is cooked, remove from the pan and let cool. Decorate with chocolate curls before serving.

pear tart with chocolate sauce

SERVES 6

¾ cup all-purpose flour

¼ cup ground almonds

5 tbsp margarine, plus extra for greasing

about 3 tbsp water

filling

4 tbsp butter

¼ cup superfine sugar

2 eggs, beaten

1 cup ground almonds

2 tbsp unsweetened cocoa

a few drops of almond extract

14 oz/400 g of canned pear halves in natural juice, drained

chocolate sauce

¼ cup superfine sugar

3 tbsp dark corn syrup

generous ⅓ cup water

6 oz/175 g semisweet chocolate, broken into pieces

2 tbsp butter

1 Preheat the oven to 400°F/200°C. Grease an 8-inch/20-cm round tart pan.

2 Sift the flour into a mixing bowl and stir in the ground almonds. Rub in the margarine with your fingertips until the mixture resembles breadcrumbs. Add enough of the water to mix to a soft dough. Cover and chill in the freezer for 10 minutes, then roll out and use to line the prepared pan. Prick the bottom with a fork and chill in the freezer for an additional 10 minutes.

3 To make the filling, beat the butter and sugar until light and fluffy. Beat in the eggs, then fold in the ground almonds, cocoa, and almond extract. Spread the chocolate mixture over the bottom of the pastry shell. Thinly slice the pears widthwise, flatten slightly, then arrange the slices on top of the chocolate mixture, pressing down lightly. Bake in the preheated oven for 30 minutes, or until the filling has risen. Cool slightly and transfer to a serving dish, if you want.

4 To make the chocolate sauce, place the sugar, corn syrup, and water in a saucepan and heat gently, stirring until the sugar dissolves. Simmer gently for 1 minute. Remove from the heat, add the chocolate and butter, and stir until melted. Serve with the tart.

chocolate apple lattice tart

SERVES 6

scant 1½ cups all-purpose flour, plus extra for dusting

2 tbsp unsweetened cocoa

scant ½ cup unsalted butter, diced, plus extra for greasing

3 tbsp superfine sugar

1–2 egg yolks, beaten

filling

1 cup heavy cream

2 eggs, beaten

1 tsp ground cinnamon

4 oz/115 g semisweet chocolate, grated

4 apples, peeled, sliced, and brushed with lemon juice

3 tbsp raw sugar

1 To make the pie dough, sift the flour and cocoa into a bowl. Rub in the butter with your fingertips until the mixture resembles breadcrumbs. Stir in the sugar and mix well. Stir in enough egg yolk to form a dough. Form into a ball, wrap in foil, and chill in the refrigerator for 45 minutes.

2 Preheat the oven to 350°F/180°C. Grease an 8-inch/20-cm round loose-bottom tart pan. Roll out the dough on a lightly floured surface and use three-quarters of it to line the pan.

3 For the filling, beat together the cream, eggs (reserving a little for glazing), cinnamon, and chocolate in a bowl. Stir in the apples. Spoon into the pastry shell, then sprinkle over the raw sugar.

4 Roll out the remaining dough and cut into long, thin strips, then arrange over the tart to form a lattice pattern. Brush the pastry strips with the reserved beaten egg, then bake in the preheated oven for 40–45 minutes.

5 Remove from the oven, let cool, and serve at room temperature.

caramel chocolate puff tarts

SERVES 6

13 oz/375 g store-bought puff pastry

5 oz/140 g semisweet chocolate, broken into pieces

1¼ cups heavy cream

¼ cup superfine sugar

4 egg yolks

4 tbsp store-bought caramel sauce

whipped cream, for serving

unsweetened cocoa, for dusting

1 Line the bottoms of a 12-hole muffin pan with disks of parchment paper. Cut out 12 x 2-inch/5-cm rounds from the edge of the pastry and cut the remainder into 12 strips. Roll the strips to half their thickness and line the sides of each hole with 1 strip. Place a disk of pastry in each bottom and press together to seal and make a tart shell. Prick the bottoms and let chill in the refrigerator for 30 minutes.

2 Preheat the oven to 400°F/200°C. While the pastry is chilling, place the chocolate in a heatproof bowl, set the bowl over a saucepan of gently simmering water, and heat until melted. Let cool slightly, then stir in the cream.

3 Place the sugar and egg yolks in a bowl and beat together, then mix well with the melted chocolate. Place a teaspoonful of the caramel sauce into each tart shell, then divide the chocolate mixture evenly among the tarts.

4 Bake in the preheated oven for 20–25 minutes, turning the pan around halfway through cooking, until just set. Let cool in the pan, then remove carefully and serve with whipped cream, dusted with cocoa.

Step 1

Step 2

Step 3

chocolate crumble pie

SERVES 8

1¼ cups all-purpose flour

1 tsp baking powder

½ cup unsalted butter, diced

¼ cup superfine sugar

1 egg yolk

1–2 tsp cold water

filling

⅔ cup heavy cream

⅔ cup milk

8 oz/225 g semisweet chocolate, chopped

2 eggs

crumble topping

½ cup packed brown sugar

¾ cup toasted pecans

4 oz/115 g semisweet chocolate

18 amaretti cookies

1 tsp unsweetened cocoa

1 To make the pie dough, sift the flour and baking powder into a large bowl and rub in the butter until the mixture resembles breadcrumbs. Stir in the superfine sugar, then add the egg yolk and a little water to bring the dough together. Turn the dough out and knead briefly. Wrap the dough and let chill in the refrigerator for 30 minutes. Meanwhile, preheat the oven to 375°F/190°C.

2 Roll out the pie dough and use to line a 9-inch/23-cm round loose-bottom tart pan. Prick the pastry shell with a fork. Line with parchment paper and fill with dried beans. Bake in the preheated oven for 15 minutes. Remove from the oven and take out the paper and beans. Reduce the oven temperature to 350°F/180°C.

3 To make the filling, bring the cream and milk to a boil in a saucepan, remove from the heat, and add the chocolate. Stir until melted and smooth. Beat the eggs and add to the chocolate mixture, mix thoroughly, and pour into the pastry shell. Bake for 15 minutes, remove from the oven, and let rest for 1 hour.

4 When you are ready to serve the pie, place the brown sugar in a large bowl. Chop the pecans and chocolate with a large knife and crush the cookies, then add to the bowl with the cocoa and mix well. Sprinkle over the pie, then serve it cut into slices.

chocolate pecan pie

SERVES 6–8

1½ cups all-purpose flour, plus extra for dusting

scant 1 cup butter

1 tbsp superfine sugar

1 egg yolk, beaten with 1 tbsp water

filling

4 tbsp butter

3 tbsp unsweetened cocoa

1 cup dark corn syrup

3 eggs

½ cup dark brown sugar

1¼ cups pecans

1 To make the pie dough, sift the flour into a bowl. Rub in the butter with your fingertips until the mixture resembles breadcrumbs, stir in the superfine sugar, then add the beaten egg yolk. Knead lightly to form a firm dough. Cover and chill in the refrigerator for 1½ hours.

2 Preheat the oven to 375°F/190°C. On a lightly floured surface, roll out the pie dough and use to line an 8-inch/20-cm round tart pan. Put a cookie sheet in the oven to heat.

3 To make the filling, put the butter in a saucepan and heat gently until melted. Sift in the cocoa and add the corn syrup. Put the eggs and brown sugar in a bowl and beat together. Stir in the butter mixture and the pecans.

4 Pour the filling into the pastry shell, place on the preheated cookie sheet, and bake in the preheated oven for 35–40 minutes, until the filling is just set. Let cool slightly and serve warm.

chocolate meringue pie

SERVES 6

8 oz/225 g semisweet chocolate-covered graham crackers

4 tbsp butter

filling

3 egg yolks

¼ cup superfine sugar

¼ cup cornstarch

2½ cups milk

3½ oz/100 g semisweet chocolate, broken into pieces

meringue

2 egg whites

½ cup superfine sugar

¼ tsp vanilla extract

1 Preheat the oven to 375°F/190°C. Place the graham crackers in a plastic bag and crush with a rolling pin. Put in a bowl. Melt the butter and stir into the cracker crumbs until well combined. Press the mixture firmly into the bottom and up the sides of a 9-inch/23-cm round tart pan.

2 To make the filling, beat the egg yolks, sugar, and cornstarch in a large bowl until they form a smooth paste. Heat the milk until almost boiling, then slowly pour it onto the egg mixture, whisking well.

3 Put the filling in a saucepan and cook gently, whisking continuously until it thickens. Remove from the heat. Put the chocolate in a heatproof bowl set over a saucepan of gently simmering water until melted. Whisk the melted chocolate into the egg mixture, then pour into the graham cracker pie shell.

4 To make the meringue, whisk the egg whites in a large, grease-free bowl until soft peaks form. Gradually whisk in about two-thirds of the sugar until the mixture is stiff and glossy. Fold in the remaining sugar and the vanilla extract.

5 Spread the meringue over the filling, swirling the surface with the back of a spoon to give it an attractive finish. Bake in the preheated oven for 30 minutes, or until the meringue is golden. Serve hot or just warm.

chocolate bread pudding with hot fudge sauce

SERVES 4

6 thick slices white bread,crusts removed

scant 2 cups milk

¾ cup of canned evaporated milk

2 tbsp unsweetened cocoa

2 eggs

2 tbsp brown sugar

1 tsp vanilla extra

confectioners' sugar, for dusting

hot fudge sauce

2 oz/55 g semisweet chocolate, broken into pieces

1 tbsp unsweetened cocoa

2 tbsp light corn syrup

¼ cup butter or margarine

2 tbsp brown sugar

⅔ cup milk

1 tbsp cornstarch

1 Grease a shallow ovenproof dish. Cut the bread into squares and layer them in the dish.

2 Put the milk, evaporated milk, and unsweetened cocoa into a saucepan and heat gently, stirring occasionally, until the mixture is lukewarm. Whisk the eggs, sugar, and vanilla extract together. Add the warm milk mixture and beat well.

3 Pour into the prepared dish, making sure that all the bread is completely covered. Cover the dish with plastic wrap and let chill in the refrigerator for 1–2 hours, then bake in a preheated oven 350°F/180°C, for 35–40 minutes, until set. Let stand for 5 minutes.

4 To make the sauce, put all the ingredients into a saucepan and heat gently, stirring continuously, until smooth.

5 Dust the chocolate bread pudding with confectioners' sugar and serve immediately with the hot fudge sauce.

Step 1

Step 3

Step 4

chocolate fruit crisp

SERVES 4

14 oz/400 g of canned apricots in natural juice

3 baking apples, peeled and thickly sliced

crisp topping

¾ cup all-purpose flour

6 tbsp butter, diced, plus extra for greasing

⅔ cup rolled oats

¼ cup superfine sugar

⅔ cup semisweet or milk chocolate chips

1 Preheat the oven to 350°F/180°C. Grease an ovenproof dish.

2 Drain the apricots, reserving 4 tablespoons of the juice. Place the apples and apricots in the prepared ovenproof dish with the reserved apricot juice and toss to mix.

3 To make the crisp topping, sift the flour into a bowl and rub in the butter with your fingertips until the mixture resembles fine breadcrumbs. Stir in the rolled oats, sugar, and chocolate chips.

4 Sprinkle the crisp mixture over the apples and apricots and smooth the top. Do not press the topping into the fruit.

5 Bake in the preheated oven for 40–45 minutes, or until the topping is golden. Serve hot.

chocolate nut strudel

SERVES 6

generous $1\frac{1}{4}$ cups mixed chopped nuts

4 oz/115 g semisweet chocolate, chopped

4 oz/115 g milk chocolate, chopped

4 oz/115 g white chocolate, chopped

7 oz/200 g filo dough, thawed if frozen

$\frac{3}{4}$ cup butter, plus extra for greasing

3 tbsp dark corn syrup

1 Preheat the oven to 375°F/190°C. Grease a baking sheet.

2 Set aside 1 tablespoon of the nuts. Place the remaining nuts in a bowl and mix together with the three types of chocolate.

3 Place a sheet of filo dough on a clean dish towel. Melt the butter and brush the sheet of filo with the butter, drizzle with a little corn syrup, and sprinkle with a little of the nut-and-chocolate mixture. Repeat the layers until you have used up all the filo dough, butter, nuts, and chocolate and most of the corn syrup.

4 Use the dish towel to help you carefully roll up the strudel and place it on the baking sheet. Drizzle with a little more corn syrup, and sprinkle with the reserved nuts. Bake in the preheated oven for 20–25 minutes. If the nuts start to brown too much, cover the strudel with a sheet of foil. Serve warm.

chocolate cherry clafoutis

SERVES 6–8

butter, for greasing

3 cups pitted black cherries

2 tbsp granulated sugar

3 eggs

¼ cup superfine sugar

½ cup self-rising flour

¼ cup unsweetened cocoa

¾ cup heavy cream

1¼ cups milk

2 tbsp kirsch (optional)

lightly whipped cream, to serve

1 Preheat the oven to 375°F/190°C. Grease a 9-inch/23-cm square ovenproof dish.

2 Arrange the cherries in the prepared dish, sprinkle with the granulated sugar, and set aside.

3 Put the eggs and superfine sugar in a bowl and whisk together until light and frothy. Sift the flour and cocoa into a separate bowl and add, all at once, to the egg mixture. Beat in thoroughly, then beat in the cream followed by the milk and kirsch, if using. Pour the batter over the cherries.

4 Bake in the preheated oven for 50–60 minutes, until slightly risen and set in the center. Serve warm with cream.

blueberry chocolate pudding with rum syrup

SERVES 4

½ cup butter, softened, plus extra for greasing

⅔ cup brown sugar

2 eggs

⅔ cup all-purpose flour

½ tsp baking powder

2 tbsp unsweetened cocoa

¾ cup blueberries, plus whole blueberries to decorate

rum syrup

4 oz/115 g semisweet chocolate, chopped

2 tbsp maple syrup

1 tbsp unsalted butter

1 tbsp rum

1 Grease a large deep ovenproof bowl. Pour water into a large saucepan to a depth of 3–4 inches/7.5–10 cm and heat over low heat until simmering.

2 Put the butter, sugar, eggs, flour, baking powder, and cocoa into a large bowl and beat together until thoroughly mixed. Stir in the blueberries. Spoon the mixture into the prepared bowl and cover tightly with two layers of foil. Carefully place the bowl in the pan of simmering water, making sure that the water level is lower than the bowl's rim. Steam the pudding for 1 hour, filling up the water when necessary.

3 About 5 minutes before the end of the cooking time, heat the ingredients for the rum syrup in a small saucepan over low heat, stirring, until smooth and melted. Remove the pudding from the heat, discard the foil, and run a knife around the edge to loosen the pudding. Turn out onto a serving dish, pour over the syrup, and decorate with blueberries. Serve immediately.

chocolate crêpes with berry compote

SERVES 4–5

generous ⅔ cup all-purpose flour

scant ¼ cup unsweetened cocoa

pinch of salt

1 egg

2 tbsp superfine sugar

1½ cups milk

scant 4 tbsp unsalted butter

berry compote

1 cup fresh blackberries

1 cup fresh blueberries

1¾ cups fresh raspberries

generous ¼ cup superfine sugar

juice of ½ lemon

½ tsp allspice (optional)

1 Preheat the oven to 275°F/140°C. Sift the flour, cocoa, and salt together into a large bowl and make a well in the center. Beat the egg, sugar, and half the milk together in a separate bowl, then pour the mixture into the dry ingredients. Beat the dry ingredients into the liquid, gradually drawing them in from the side, until a batter is formed. Gradually beat in the remaining milk. Pour the batter into a pitcher.

2 Heat a 7-inch/18-cm nonstick skillet over medium heat and add about 1 tablespoon of the butter. When the butter has melted, pour in enough batter to just cover the bottom, then swirl it around the skillet so that you have a thin, even layer. Cook for 30 seconds, then lift up the edge of the crêpe to check if it is cooked. Loosen the crêpe around the edge, then flip it over with a spatula. Cook on the other side until the bottom is golden brown.

3 Transfer the crêpe to a warmed plate and keep warm in the preheated oven while you cook the remaining batter, adding the remaining butter to the skillet as necessary. Make a stack of the crêpes with parchment paper in between each one.

4 To make the compote, pick over the berries and put in a saucepan with the sugar, lemon juice, and allspice, if using. Cook over low heat until the sugar has dissolved and the berries are warmed through. Put a crêpe on a warmed serving plate and spoon some of the compote onto the center. Either roll or fold the crêpe. Repeat with the remaining crêpes.

chocolate & raspberry pavlova

SERVES 6

meringue

4 egg whites

1 cup superfine sugar

1 tsp cornstarch

1 tsp white wine vinegar

1 tsp vanilla extract

topping

1¼ cups heavy cream

1 tbsp superfine sugar

2 tbsp framboise liqueur

1 cup fresh raspberries

2 oz/55 g semisweet chocolate shavings

1 Preheat the oven to 300°F/150°C. In a large, grease-free bowl, beat the egg whites until stiff using an electric mixer, then gradually beat in a generous ½ cup of the sugar. In a separate bowl, mix the remaining sugar with the cornstarch and then beat it into the egg white mixture; it should be very shiny and firm. Quickly fold the vinegar and vanilla extract into the egg white mixture.

2 Draw a 10-inch/25-cm circle on a sheet of parchment paper, turn the paper over, and place it on a baking sheet. Pile the meringue onto the parchment paper and spread evenly to the edge of the circle; swirl it around on top to make an attractive shape. Bake in the center of the preheated oven for 1 hour.

3 Remove from the oven, let cool slightly, then peel off the paper. Place the meringue on a large serving plate. It will shrink and crack, but do not worry about this.

4 An hour before serving, whip together the cream, sugar, and liqueur until thick and floppy. Pile on top of the meringue and decorate with the raspberries and chocolate shavings. Chill before serving.

cream puffs with chocolate sauce

SERVES 4

choux pastry

5 tbsp butter, plus extra for greasing

scant 1 cup water

¾ cup all-purpose flour

3 eggs, beaten

cream filling

1¼ cups heavy cream

3 tbsp superfine sugar

1 tsp vanilla extract

chocolate sauce

4½ oz/125 g semisweet chocolate, broken into small pieces

2½ tbsp butter

6 tbsp water

2 tbsp cognac

1 Preheat the oven to 400°F/200°C. Grease a large baking sheet.

2 To make the choux pastry, place the butter and water in a saucepan and bring to a boil. Meanwhile, sift the flour into a bowl. Turn off the heat and beat the flour into the liquid until smooth. Cool for 5 minutes. Beat in enough of the beaten egg to give the mixture a soft, dropping consistency.

3 Transfer to a pastry bag fitted with a ½-inch/1-cm plain tip. Pipe small balls onto the prepared baking sheet. Bake in the preheated oven for 25 minutes. Remove from the oven. Pierce each ball with a toothpick to let the steam escape.

4 To make the filling, whip the cream, sugar, and vanilla extract together. Cut the balls across the middle, then fill with the cream mixture.

5 To make the sauce, gently melt the chocolate, butter, and water together in a small saucepan, stirring continuously, until smooth. Stir in the cognac.

6 Pile the cream puffs into individual serving dishes, pour over the sauce, and serve.

raspberry & white chocolate brûlées

SERVES 6

7 oz/200 g white chocolate, broken into pieces

scant 1 cup light cream

2 cups Greek-style yogurt

1¾ cups raspberries

⅓ cup granulated sugar

3 tbsp water

1 Place the chocolate and light cream in a heatproof bowl. Set the bowl over a saucepan of simmering water and heat, stirring occasionally, until melted and smooth. Remove from the heat and let cool slightly.

2 Stir the chocolate mixture into the yogurt, then fold in the raspberries. Divide between 6 x ⅔ cup heatproof dishes or ramekins and level the tops with the back of a teaspoon. Chill in the refrigerator for at least 30 minutes.

3 Place the granulated sugar and water in a small heavy-bottom saucepan. Heat gently until the sugar dissolves, then turn up the heat and boil rapidly, for about 4 minutes, without stirring, until the sugar turns a rich caramel color.

4 Remove from the heat and let the bubbles subside, then quickly spoon some caramel over the top of each brûlée. It will set almost immediately. Serve immediately, or chill and serve within 3 hours while the caramel is still crisp.

Step 1

Step 2

Step 2

white chocolate tiramisu

SERVES 4

16 ladyfingers

1 cup strong black coffee, cooled to room temperature

4 tbsp almond-flavored liqueur, such as amaretto

9 oz/250 g mascarpone cheese

1¼ cups heavy cream

3 tbsp superfine sugar

4½ oz/125 g white chocolate, grated

¼ cup toasted slivered almonds, to decorate

1 Break the ladyfingers into pieces and divide half of them equally among 4 serving glasses. Mix the coffee and liqueur together in a pitcher, then pour half over the ladyfingers in the glasses.

2 Beat the mascarpone, cream, sugar, and just less than half of the chocolate together in a bowl. Spread half the mixture over the coffee-soaked ladyfingers, then arrange the remaining ladyfingers on top. Pour over the remaining coffee mixture, then spread over the remaining cream mixture. Sprinkle with the remaining chocolate.

3 Cover with plastic wrap and chill in the refrigerator for at least 2 hours, or until required. Sprinkle over the slivered almonds before serving.

chocolate trifle

SERVES 8

10 oz/280 g store-bought chocolate loaf cake

3–4 tbsp seedless raspberry jelly

4 tbsp amaretto

2 cups mixed berries, such as raspberries and strawberries, thawed if frozen

chocolate truffles and chocolate shapes, to decorate

chocolate custard

6 egg yolks

¼ cup superfine sugar

1 tbsp cornstarch

2 cups milk

2 oz/55 g semisweet chocolate, broken into pieces

topping

1 cup heavy cream

1 tbsp superfine sugar

½ tsp vanilla extract

1 Cut the cake into slices and make "sandwiches" with the raspberry jelly. Cut the "sandwiches" into cubes and place in a large glass serving bowl. Sprinkle with the amaretto. Spread the berries over the cake.

2 To make the custard, put the egg yolks and sugar in a bowl and whisk until thick and pale. Stir in the cornstarch. Put the milk in a saucepan and heat until almost boiling. Pour onto the egg yolk mixture, stirring. Return the mixture to the saucepan and bring just to a boil, stirring continuously, until it thickens. Remove from the heat and let cool slightly.

3 Melt the chocolate in a heatproof bowl set over a saucepan of gently simmering water, then add to the custard. Pour over the cake and berries. Let cool, then cover with plastic wrap and let chill in the refrigerator for 2 hours, or until set.

4 To make the topping, put the cream in a bowl and whip until soft peaks form. Beat in the sugar and vanilla extract. Spoon over the trifle. Decorate with truffles and chocolate shapes and chill until ready to serve.

chocolate parfait sandwiches

SERVES 4

3 extra-large egg whites

¾ cup superfine sugar

5 oz/140 g white chocolate, grated

1¾ cups cream, whipped

12 oz/350 g puff pastry

melted semisweet chocolate, to decorate

1 To make the parfait, beat the egg whites and the sugar together in a heatproof bowl, then set the bowl over a saucepan of gently simmering water. Using an electric handheld mixer, beat the whites over the heat until you have a light and fluffy meringue. This will take up to 10 minutes. Remove from the heat, add the chocolate, and keep beating to cool. Fold in the whipped cream.

2 Spoon the parfait into a shallow, rectangular freezerproof container and freeze for 5–6 hours.

3 Meanwhile, preheat the oven to 350°F/180°C and line a cookie sheet with parchment paper. Cut the puff pastry into regular-size rectangles to accommodate a slice of the parfait. Place the puff pastry rectangles on the sheet and top with another cookie sheet, which will keep the puff pastry flat but crisp. Bake in the preheated oven for 15 minutes, transfer to a wire rack, and let cool.

4 About 20 minutes before you are ready to serve, remove the parfait from the freezer. When it has softened, cut the parfait into slices and put each slice between 2 pieces of puff pastry to make a "sandwich." Drizzle with the melted chocolate.

white chocolate terrine

SERVES 8

2 tbsp granulated sugar

5 tbsp water

10 oz/280 g white chocolate, broken into pieces

3 eggs, separated

1¼ cups heavy cream

fruit coulis and fresh strawberries, to serve

1 Line an 8 x 4 x 2-inch/20 x 10 x 5-cm loaf pan with plastic wrap, pressing out as many creases as you can.

2 Place the sugar and water in a heavy-bottom saucepan and heat gently, stirring, until the sugar has dissolved. Bring to a boil and boil for 1–2 minutes, until syrupy, then remove from the heat.

3 Stir the chocolate pieces into the hot syrup, continuing to stir until the chocolate has melted and combined with the syrup. Let the mixture cool slightly. Beat the egg yolks into the chocolate mixture. Let cool completely.

4 Lightly whip the cream until it is just holding its shape, then fold it into the chocolate mixture. Whip the egg whites in a grease-free bowl until soft peaks form. Fold into the chocolate mixture. Pour into the prepared loaf pan and freeze overnight.

5 To serve, remove the terrine from the freezer about 10–15 minutes before serving. Turn out of the pan and cut into slices. Serve with fruit coulis and strawberries.

VARIATION

This terrine could also be served with the chocolate sauce from page 120, instead of the fruit coulis.

4

Special Treats

chocolate banana sundae

SERVES 4

chocolate sauce

2 oz/55 g semisweet chocolate

4 tbsp dark corn syrup

1 tbsp butter

1 tbsp cognac or dark rum (optional)

sundae

⅔ cup heavy cream

4 bananas, peeled

8 scoops good-quality vanilla ice cream

¾ cup chopped mixed nuts, toasted

1½ oz/40 g milk or semisweet chocolate, grated

4 ice-cream fan wafers, to serve

1 To make the chocolate sauce, break the chocolate into small pieces and place in a heatproof bowl with the corn syrup and butter. Set over a saucepan of gently simmering water until melted, stirring until well combined. Remove the bowl from the heat and stir in the cognac, if using.

2 Whip the cream until just holding its shape, and slice the bananas. Place a scoop of ice cream in the bottom of each of four sundae glasses. Top with slices of banana, some chocolate sauce, a spoonful of cream, and a generous sprinkling of nuts.

3 Repeat the layers, finishing with a good dollop of cream, then sprinkle with the remaining nuts and the grated chocolate. Top each sundae with a fan wafer.

chocolate chip ice cream

SERVES 4–6

1¼ cups milk

1 vanilla bean

4 oz/115 g milk chocolate

scant ½ cup superfine sugar

3 egg yolks

1¼ cups heavy cream

ice-cream cones, to serve

1 Pour the milk into a heavy saucepan, add the vanilla bean, and bring almost to a boil. Remove from the heat and let stand for 30 minutes. Meanwhile, chop the chocolate into small pieces and set aside.

2 Put the sugar and egg yolks in a large bowl and whisk together until pale and the mixture leaves a trail when the whisk is lifted. Remove the vanilla bean from the milk, then gradually add the milk to the sugar mixture, stirring continuously with a wooden spoon. Strain the mixture into the rinsed-out pan and cook over low heat for 10–15 minutes, stirring continuously, until the mixture thickens enough to coat the back of the wooden spoon. Do not let the mixture boil or it will curdle. Remove from the heat, cover, and let cool for at least 1 hour, stirring occasionally to prevent a skin from forming. Meanwhile, whip the cream until it holds its shape. Set aside in the refrigerator until ready to use.

3 If using an ice-cream machine, fold the whipped cream into the cold custard, then churn the mixture in the machine following the manufacturer's instructions. Just before the ice cream freezes, add the chocolate pieces. Alternatively, freeze the custard in a freezerproof container, uncovered, for 1–2 hours, until beginning to set around the edges. Turn the custard into a bowl and stir with a fork or beat in a food processor until smooth. Fold in the whipped cream and chocolate pieces. Return to the freezer and freeze for an additional 2–3 hours, or until firm. Scoop the ice cream into cones to serve.

layered chocolate mousse

SERVES 6

3 eggs

1 tsp cornstarch

¼ cups superfine sugar

1¼ cups milk

1 envelope powdered gelatin

3 tbsp water

1¼ cups heavy cream

2¾ oz/75 g semisweet chocolate, broken into pieces

2¾ oz/75 g white chocolate, broken into pieces

2¾ oz/75 g milk chocolate, broken into pieces

chocolate curls, to decorate

1 Line a 9 x 5 x 3-inch/23 x 13 x 8-cm loaf pan with plastic wrap. Separate the eggs, putting each egg white in a separate bowl. Place the egg yolks, cornstarch, and sugar in a large heatproof bowl and whisk until well combined. Place the milk in a saucepan and heat gently, stirring until almost boiling. Pour the milk onto the egg yolk mixture, whisking.

2 Set the bowl over a saucepan of gently simmering water and cook, stirring until the mixture thickens enough to thinly coat the back of a wooden spoon. Sprinkle the gelatin over the water in a small heatproof bowl and let it turn spongy. Set over a saucepan of hot water and stir until dissolved. Stir into the hot custard mixture. Let the mixture cool.

3 Whip the cream until just holding its shape. Fold into the custard, then divide the mixture into 3. Put the 3 types of chocolate in separate heatproof bowls set over saucepans of gently simmering water until melted. Fold the semisweet chocolate into 1 custard portion. Whisk 1 of the egg whites until soft peaks form and fold into the semisweet chocolate custard until combined. Pour into the prepared pan and smooth the top. Chill in the coldest part of the refrigerator until just set. Keep the other mixtures at room temperature.

4 Fold the white chocolate into another portion of the custard. Whisk another egg white and fold in. Pour on top of the semisweet chocolate layer and chill quickly. Repeat with the milk chocolate and the remaining egg white. Chill for at least 2 hours, until set. To serve, carefully turn out onto a serving dish and decorate with chocolate curls.

chocolate ice cream pops

SERVES 6

$2\frac{1}{2}$ cups good-quality vanilla ice cream

7 oz/200 g semisweet chocolate

2 tbsp unsalted butter

1 Line a cookie sheet with parchment paper.

2 Using a melon baller, scoop out balls of ice cream and place them on the prepared cookie sheet. Alternatively, cut the ice cream into bite-size cubes. Stick a toothpick in each piece and return to the freezer until very hard.

3 Place the chocolate and the butter in a heatproof bowl set over a saucepan of gently simmering water until melted. Quickly dip the frozen ice-cream balls into the warm chocolate, place in a muffin cup, and return to the freezer to set. Keep them there until ready to serve.

Step 2

Step 3

Step 3

chocolate hazelnut pots

SERVES 4

2 eggs

2 egg yolks

1 tbsp superfine sugar

1 tsp cornstarch

2½ cups milk

3 oz/85 g semisweet chocolate, broken into pieces

¼ cup chocolate hazelnut spread

lightly whipped cream and chocolate curls, to decorate

1 Preheat the oven to 325°F/160°C. Beat together the eggs, egg yolks, superfine sugar, and cornstarch until well combined. Heat the milk until it is almost boiling. Gradually pour the milk onto the eggs, whisking as you do so.

2 Melt the semisweet chocolate and chocolate hazelnut spread in a heatproof bowl set over a saucepan of gently simmering water, then whisk the melted chocolate mixture into the egg mixture.

3 Pour into 4 small ovenproof dishes and cover the dishes with foil. Place them in a roasting pan. Fill the pan with boiling water until halfway up the sides of the dishes. Bake in the preheated oven for 35–40 minutes, until just set.

4 Remove from the pan and let cool, then chill until required. Serve decorated with whipped cream and chocolate curls.

chocolate rum pots

SERVES 6

8 oz/225 g semisweet chocolate, broken into pieces

4 eggs, separated

⅓ cup superfine sugar

4 tbsp dark rum

4 tbsp heavy cream

whipped cream and marbled chocolate shapes, to decorate

1 Put the chocolate in a heatproof bowl set over a saucepan of gently simmering water until melted. Let cool slightly.

2 Whisk the egg yolks with the sugar in a bowl until very pale and fluffy. Drizzle the melted chocolate into the mixture and fold in together with the rum and the cream.

3 Whisk the egg whites in a grease-free bowl until soft peaks form. Fold the egg whites into the chocolate mixture in two batches. Divide the mixture among six serving dishes and let chill in the refrigerator for at least 2 hours.

4 To serve, decorate with a little whipped cream and top with marbled chocolate shapes.

chocolate zabaglione

SERVES 4

4 egg yolks

¼ cup superfine sugar

1¾ oz/50 g semisweet chocolate

½ cup marsala wine

unsweetened cocoa, for dusting

1 Place the egg yolks and sugar in a large heatproof bowl and beat together, using a handheld electric mixer, until the mixture is very pale.

2 Grate the chocolate finely and fold into the egg mixture. Fold in the marsala wine.

3 Place the bowl over a saucepan of gently simmering water and set the electric mixer on the lowest speed or swap to a balloon whisk. Cook gently, beating continuously, until the mixture thickens. Do not overcook or the mixture will curdle.

4 Spoon the hot mixture into four heatproof glasses and dust with cocoa. Serve as soon as possible, while it is warm, light, and fluffy.

chocolate fondue

SERVES 6

1 pineapple

1 mango

9 oz/250 g fresh strawberries

9 oz/250 g seedless green grapes

fondue

9 oz/250 g semisweet chocolate, broken into pieces

⅔ cup heavy cream

2 tbsp cognac

1 Using a sharp knife, peel and core the pineapple, then cut the flesh into cubes. Peel the mango, remove the pit, and cut the flesh into cubes. Arrange all the fruit on six serving plates and let chill in the refrigerator.

2 To make the fondue, place the chocolate and cream in a fondue pot. Heat gently, stirring continuously, until the chocolate has melted. Stir in the cognac until thoroughly blended and the chocolate mixture is smooth.

3 Place the fondue pot over the burner to keep warm. To serve, let each guest dip the fruit into the fondue, using fondue forks or bamboo skewers.

Step 1

Step 1

Step 2

italian chocolate truffles

MAKES 24

6 oz/175 g semisweet chocolate, broken into pieces

2 tbsp amaretto liqueur or orange-flavored liqueur

3 tbsp unsalted butter

¼ cup confectioners' sugar

½ cup ground almonds

1¾ oz/50 g semisweet chocolate, grated, to decorate

1 Melt the chocolate with the liqueur in a heatproof bowl set over a saucepan of gently simmering water, stirring until well combined.

2 Add the butter and stir until it has melted. Stir in the sugar and the ground almonds.

3 Let the mixture stand in a cool place until it is firm enough to roll into 24 balls.

4 Place the grated chocolate on a plate and roll the truffles in the chocolate to coat them.

5 Place the truffles in paper candy cups and let chill in the refrigerator.

white chocolate truffles

MAKES 20

2 tbsp unsalted butter

5 tbsp heavy cream

12 oz/350 g white chocolate, broken into pieces

1 tbsp orange-flavored liqueur (optional)

1 Line a jelly roll pan with parchment paper. Place the butter and cream in a small saucepan and bring slowly to a boil, stirring continuously. Boil for 1 minute, then remove from the heat.

2 Add 8 oz/225 g of the chocolate to the cream. Stir until melted, then beat in the liqueur, if using. Pour into the prepared pan and chill in the refrigerator for about 2 hours, until firm.

3 Break off pieces of the mixture and roll them into 20 balls. Chill for an additional 30 minutes.

4 To finish, put the remaining chocolate in a heatproof bowl set over a saucepan of gently simmering water until melted. Using 2 forks, carefully dip the balls into the chocolate, letting the excess drip back into the bowl. Place on parchment paper, swirl the chocolate with the tines of a fork, and let set.

chocolate creams

MAKES 30

7 oz/200 g semisweet chocolate, broken into pieces

2 tbsp light cream

2 cups confectioners' sugar

drinking chocolate powder, for dusting

1 Line a cookie sheet with parchment paper. Melt 2 oz/55 g of the chocolate in a large heatproof bowl set over a saucepan of gently simmering water. Stir in the cream and remove the bowl from the heat.

2 Sift the confectioners' sugar into the melted chocolate mixture, then, using a fork, mix well together. Knead to form a firm, smooth, pliable mixture.

3 Lightly dust a surface with drinking chocolate powder, turn out the mixture, and roll out to a thickness of ¼ inch/5 mm. Cut into circles using a 1-inch/2.5-cm plain round cutter.

4 Transfer to the prepared cookie sheet and let stand for about 12 hours, or overnight, until set and dry.

5 When the chocolate creams have set, melt the remaining chocolate in a heatproof bowl set over a saucepan of gently simmering water. Using 2 forks, carefully dip each chocolate cream into the melted chocolate. Lift out quickly, letting any excess chocolate drip back into the bowl, then place back on the cookie sheet. Let set.

chocolate coconut ice

MAKES 50

oil, for greasing

14 oz/400 g of canned condensed milk

1 tsp vanilla extract

3¼ cups unsweetened dried shredded coconut

3⅓ cups confectioners' sugar

3 tbsp unsweetened cocoa, sifted

few drops of red food or pink food coloring (optional)

1 Grease and line the bottom of a shallow 7-inch/18-cm square cake pan with parchment paper. Mix the condensed milk and vanilla extract together in a large bowl. Add the coconut and confectioners' sugar. Mix together with a wooden spoon until the mixture becomes very stiff.

2 Transfer half of the mixture to another bowl. Add the unsweetened cocoa and mix well until it is an even color. Spread over the bottom of the prepared pan and press down with the back of a spoon.

3 If using food coloring, mix a few drops into the remaining bowl of mixture until evenly pink in color. Spread over the chocolate layer and smooth the top. Let set overnight before turning out and cutting into squares.

Step 1

Step 2

Step 3

peppermint creams

MAKES 38

1 egg white

3 cups confectioners' sugar, plus extra for dusting

a few drops of peppermint extract

7 oz/200 g semisweet chocolate, broken into pieces

1 Line a cookie sheet with a sheet of parchment paper.

2 Whisk the egg white until stiff. Gradually sift in the sugar and mix together to form a firm, pliable mixture. Add the peppermint extract to taste and mix well together.

3 Lightly dust a surface with sugar, turn out the mixture, and knead for 2–3 minutes. Roll out to a thickness of ¼ inch/5 mm, then cut into circles using a 1½-inch/4-cm plain round cutter.

4 Transfer to the prepared cookie sheet and let stand for about 24 hours, or overnight, until set and dry.

5 Melt the chocolate in a heatproof bowl set over a saucepan of gently simmering water. When the peppermints have set, carefully dip each one into the melted chocolate using 2 forks. Lift it out quickly, letting any excess chocolate drip back into the bowl, and place on the prepared cookie sheet. Let set.

chocolate cherries

MAKES 24

12 candied cherries

2 tbsp dark rum or cognac

9 oz/250 g marzipan

5½ oz/150 g semisweet chocolate, broken into pieces

milk, semisweet, or white chocolate, to decorate

1 Line a cookie sheet with a sheet of parchment paper.

2 Cut the cherries in half and place in a small bowl. Add the rum and stir to coat. Let the cherries soak for at least 1 hour, stirring occasionally.

3 Divide the marzipan into 24 pieces and roll each piece into a ball. Press half a cherry into the top of each marzipan ball.

4 Put the chocolate in a heatproof bowl set over a saucepan of gently simmering water. Stir until all the chocolate has melted.

5 Dip each marzipan ball into the melted chocolate using a toothpick, letting the excess drip back into the bowl. Place the marzipan balls on the prepared cookie sheet and chill until set.

6 Melt a little extra chocolate and drizzle it over the top of the coated cherries to decorate. Let set.

ginger chocolate fudge

MAKES 50

6 pieces preserved ginger, plus extra to decorate

1¼ cups milk

5½ oz/150 g semisweet chocolate, broken into pieces

½ cup unsalted butter, plus extra for greasing

2⅓ cups granulated sugar

1 Grease a 7-inch/18-cm square cake pan or an 8 x 6-inch/20 x 15-cm cake pan. Dry the syrup off the pieces of preserved ginger on paper towels, then chop finely.

2 Pour the milk into a large heavy-bottom saucepan and add the chocolate, butter, and sugar. Heat gently, stirring all the time, until the chocolate and butter have melted and the sugar has dissolved.

3 Bring to a boil, then boil for 10–15 minutes, stirring occasionally, until a little of the mixture, dropped into a small bowl of cold water, forms a soft ball when rolled between your fingers.

4 Remove the saucepan from the heat and stir in the chopped ginger. Let cool for 5 minutes, then beat the mixture vigorously with a wooden spoon until thick, creamy, and grainy.

5 Immediately pour the mixture into the prepared pan, let cool, then mark into small squares. Let the fudge stand until set, then cut up the squares with a sharp knife. Decorate with pieces of preserved ginger.

pecan mocha fudge

MAKES 80

$1\frac{1}{4}$ cups milk

8 cups granulated sugar

generous 1 cup butter, plus extra for greasing

2 tbsp instant coffee granules

2 tbsp unsweetened cocoa

2 tbsp corn syrup

14 oz/400 g of canned condensed milk

½ cup shelled pecans, chopped

1 Grease a 12 x 9-inch/30 x 23-cm jelly roll pan. Place the milk, sugar, and butter in a large saucepan. Stir over gentle heat until the sugar has dissolved. Stir in the coffee granules, cocoa, corn syrup, and condensed milk.

2 Bring to a boil and boil steadily, whisking continuously, for 10 minutes, or until a temperature of 240°F/115°C has been reached on a sugar thermometer, or a small amount of the mixture forms a soft ball when dropped into cold water.

3 Let cool for 5 minutes, then beat vigorously with a wooden spoon until the mixture starts to thicken. Stir in the nuts. Continue beating until the mixture takes on a fudgelike consistency. Quickly pour into the prepared pan and let stand in a cool place to set. Cut the fudge into squares to serve.

Step 1

Step 2

Step 3

fruit & nut fudge

MAKES 36

9 oz/250 g semisweet chocolate, broken into pieces

2 tbsp unsalted butter, plus extra for greasing

4 tbsp evaporated milk

3 cups confectioners' sugar, sifted

½ cup coarsely chopped hazelnuts

⅓ cup golden raisins

1 Grease an 8-inch/20-cm square cake pan. Put the chocolate in a heatproof bowl with the butter and evaporated milk and set over a saucepan of gently simmering water. Stir until the chocolate and butter have melted and the mixture is well blended.

2 Remove the bowl from the heat and gradually beat in the confectioners' sugar. Stir the hazelnuts and golden raisins into the mixture. Press the fudge into the prepared pan and smooth the top. Chill in the refrigerator until firm.

3 Turn the fudge out onto a cutting board and cut into squares. Chill in the refrigerator until ready to serve.

brazil nut brittle

MAKES 20

sunflower oil, for brushing

12 oz/350 g semisweet chocolate, broken into pieces

scant ¾ cup chopped Brazil nuts

6 oz/175 g white chocolate, coarsely chopped

6 oz/175 g store-bought fudge, coarsely chopped

1. Brush the bottom of an 8-inch/20-cm square cake pan with oil and line with parchment paper.

2. Melt the semisweet chocolate in a heatproof bowl over a saucepan of gently simmering water and spread half over the bottom of the prepared pan.

3. Sprinkle with the Brazil nuts, white chocolate, and fudge. Pour the remaining melted chocolate over the top.

4. Let set, then break up into jagged pieces using the tip of a strong knife.

chocolate milk shake

SERVES 4

1¼ cups milk

2 tbsp chocolate syrup

2 tbsp coffee syrup

6 cups chocolate ice cream

to decorate

⅔ cup heavy cream, whipped

unsweetened cocoa, for dusting

1 Pour the milk, chocolate syrup, and coffee syrup into a food processor and gently process until blended. Add the ice cream and process to a smooth consistency. Pour into four large glasses.

2 To decorate, spoon the cream into a pastry bag fitted with a large star-shaped tip. Pipe generous amounts of cream on top of the milk shakes. Sprinkle over the cocoa and serve with straws.

mocha cream

SERVES 2

generous ¾ cup milk

scant ¼ cup light cream

1 tbsp brown sugar

2 tbsp unsweetened cocoa

1 tbsp coffee syrup

6 ice cubes

whipped cream and grated chocolate, to decorate

1 Put the milk, cream, and sugar into a food processor and process gently to combine.

2 Add the cocoa and coffee syrup and process, then add the ice and process until smooth.

3 Pour into glasses. Top with whipped cream and scatter with grated chocolate.

Step 1

Step 2

Step 3

real hot chocolate

SERVES 1–2

1½ oz/40 g semisweet chocolate, broken into pieces

1¼ cups milk

chocolate curls, to decorate

1 Place the chocolate in a large heatproof pitcher. Place the milk in a heavy-bottom saucepan and bring to a boil. Pour about one-quarter of the milk onto the chocolate and let stand until the chocolate has softened.

2 Whisk the milk-and-chocolate mixture until smooth. Return the remaining milk to the heat and return to a boil, then pour onto the chocolate mixture, whisking continuously.

3 Pour into warmed mugs or cups and top with the chocolate curls. Serve immediately.

chocolate

cool minty chocolate

SERVES 4

2½ cups ice-cold milk

6 tbsp drinking chocolate powder

1 cup light cream

1 tsp peppermint extract

4 scoops chocolate-mint ice cream

fresh mint sprigs, to decorate

1 Pour half the milk into a small saucepan and stir in the drinking chocolate powder. Heat gently, stirring continuously, until just below boiling point and the mixture is smooth. Remove the saucepan from the heat.

2 Pour the chocolate-flavored milk into a large chilled bowl and whisk in the remaining milk. Whisk in the cream and peppermint extract.

3 Pour the mixture into four glasses, top each with a scoop of ice cream, and decorate with a mint sprig. Serve immediately.

chili hot chocolate

SERVES 4

2 cups milk

4 oz /115 g semisweet chocolate, broken into pieces

large pinch of chili powder, or to taste

½ tsp grated orange zest

freshly grated nutmeg, for dusting

1 Put the milk and the chocolate pieces into a small saucepan and place over low heat. Whisk the mixture together continuously, until the chocolate melts and the mixture starts to simmer.

2 Whisk in the chili powder and orange zest. Pour into cups, dust with nutmeg, and serve.

hot chocolate float

SERVES 4

2 cups milk

8 oz/225 g semisweet chocolate, broken into pieces

2 tbsp superfine sugar

8 scoops coconut ice cream

8 scoops chocolate ice cream

whipped cream, to decorate

1 Pour the milk into a saucepan. Add the chocolate pieces and the sugar to the pan. Stir over low heat until the chocolate has melted, the sugar has dissolved, and the mixture is smooth. Remove the saucepan from the heat.

2 Put 1 scoop of coconut ice cream into each of four heatproof glasses, top with a scoop of chocolate ice cream, then repeat the layers.

3 Pour the chocolate-flavored milk into the glasses, top with whipped cream, and serve immediately.

VARIATION

Instead of chocolate ice cream, use 8 marshmallows instead.